RECOVERY COACH MASTERY

DISCLAIMER: The approaches and training concepts which are written in this handbook have been conducted by Starting Point Recovery Coaching Academy and have been confirmed by both clients and professionals as effective practices. We assume no responsibility for any event that may occur as a result of anyone, professional or otherwise, using the enclosed information for treatment purposes. The information contained herein is not meant to take the place of a doctor, psychiatrist, or treatment professional. The sole purpose of the information provided is to inform behavioral health, peer and professional specialists about evidence-based techniques that have worked when coaching clients struggling with aftercare of addictive behaviors, and when used properly qualifies the trainee for certification as a Certified Recovery Coach.

If YOU DON'T LIKE WHAT YOU'RE GETTING, CHANGE WHAT YOU'RE DOING.

(Life's story in Five Easy Chapters)

Chapter One

I walk down the street. There is a deep hole in the sidewalk. I fall in. I am lost and helpless. It isn't my fault. It takes me a long time to get out.

Chapter Two

I walk down the same street. I see the same deep hole in the sidewalk. I pretend not to see it, but I fall in again. I can't believe I'm in the same place. It takes me a long time to get out.

Chapter Three

I walk down the same street. I see the same deep hole in the sidewalk. I try to avoid it, but I still fall in. I knew I would fall in, but it's a habit. I've been here before, so I get out immediately.

Chapter Four

I walk down the same street. I see the same deep hole in the sidewalk. I walk around it, but what if someday I forget it's there?

Chapter Five

I walk down a different street.

(Adapted from *"There's a Hole in My sidewalk"* by Portia Nelson)

TABLE OF CONTENTS

ACKNOWLEDGEMENTS

Starting Point dedicates this training program to every young man and woman who has ever taken a brief detour in life through addictive behaviors and who have allowed me the privilege of helping them discover options and better ways of living. To them I can only say, *"Don't become complacent in your sober journey. There will never be a third shot at a second chance."*

I am indebted to the remarkable community of treatment and aftercare recovery professionals listed in the sources and references section for dedicating their lives to understanding, treating and educating others about this baffling and powerful disease. I thank them in advance for allowing me the privilege of using cited portions of their contributions in the development of this training handbook.

To the memory of the late Earnie Larsen, who taught us the simple truths about life in recovery through his books and recorded teachings. His recovery principles have provided insight and inspiration and have served as a guide through my personal tipping moments and turning points. I wish I could have met him, yet through his works, I feel like I knew him.

A special thanks to the reviewers and editors Shira Goldberg, Barry Kinneberg, and especially Merle Bell, who in the wee hours of the night made my ramblings make better sense.

Last, I give all the credit to my Creator for granting my time on earth and for the privilege of sharing these pages with you.

Louis D. Gonzales, Ph.D.

About The Trainer

Who am I to be conducting this training? I am a behaviorist who has been pursuing the issues of reducing the recidivism rates of criminally-prone youth, and am also in the business of helping young men and women who are in need of rebuilding a life that was lost through addiction and other maladaptive behaviors.

I am a Recovery Coach, not a therapist. I have been professionally educated and trained in behavioral theory and have been coaching others for growth for over twenty years. The clients I work with are highly motivated and desire additional support and accountability to help them achieve their goal of a healthier, drug-free lifestyle. My job is to listen, guide and ask the right questions.

In past years, I have taught, supported, and persuaded people into the light in their time of despair, and in that process, I knew that there was a great need for a voice of common sense that could stand alongside them, provide direction, and create possibilities. It wasn't called coaching then, but today I am convinced that's what it was.

My initial steps toward cognitive approaches began while working on my undergraduate degree and volunteering at a counseling clinic. I began to see and understand the important changes that something as basic as telephone interactions brought about in people's lives. I quickly realized that I wanted to become professionally involved in some aspects of that process.

While working on my Master's degree in Counseling and Psychology, I was incredibly fortunate to have studied under Dr. Marilyn Bates at the State

University of California. While there, I was exposed to such great guest lecturers as Albert Ellis, William Glaser, Aaron T. Beck and others who pioneered the idea that almost all behaviors are chosen and that we alone control our feelings, not external sources; revolutionary notions for those times. Today, those very notions have evolved into best-practice principles of recovery coaching.

This initially led me to varied experiences in volunteer and statutory agencies such as public education, the Job Training Partnership Act (JTPA) employment programs, mental health agencies, the juvenile justice system, and higher education during which I worked with many diverse groups of people in many challenging situations. I then went on to earn a Ph.D. in Health and Human Services with a focus on community care.

As a result of my doctoral work came the recognition of a need for community-based programming that could provide the treatment field and professionals affiliated with the justice system, an excellent aftercare resource. From that recognition, I created several storefront alternative schools for young people not in the mainstream of education or society, and soon after *Starting Point Recovery Coaching* was established.

I have seen the pained faces of many wounded souls, and know that without our help, their recovery journey can be a long one. So here I am; richly experienced; highly educated, but still curious, probing for answers, and always learning. I'm honored to have this opportunity to share with you what I have learned and support you in your mission of helping others.

| **Member and Affiliate:** |
| Sober Network. |
| Recovery Coach International. |
| International Coach Federation. |
| National Association of Alcoholism and Drug Abuse Counselors (NAADAC). |

RECOVERY COACH MASTERY

Welcome to Starting Point's ***Recovery Coach Mastery,*** a powerful recovery and life coaching system. The name *system* refers to techniques and strategies which have been integrated into a combination of systematic, evidence-based practices used with clients recovering from addictive substances and behaviors.

William White, a major leader in the substance abuse and aftercare recovery movement once wrote: *"New service roles seem to always sprout from the soil of unmet needs."* Today, that unmet need is affordable and effective aftercare; and that new service is *Recovery Coaching.*

We have all witnessed the constant media parade of young celebrities heading back to rehab after their latest falls from grace. Today, eighty percent of persons leaving addiction treatment centers relapse within their first year following discharge and nine out of ten of those eighty percent relapse within the first ninety days. This has now produced a public that has become skeptical and unsure of exactly what *recovery* really means and whether it is attainable for all or reserved for only the financially privileged and other few exceptions. Add to this the fact that private and public monies for treatment have dried up and with the revolving door that traditional aftercare models have become, it is no wonder that professionals in the treatment field are beginning to look at other more effective resources for long-term recovery support. Out of this harsh, philosophical reality, recovery coaching was borne.

HOW THE HANDBOOK IS USED

Recovery Coach Mastery will provide you with the comprehensive skills and techniques that few recovery coach training programs have been able to provide. Recovery Coach Mastery's handbook serves as your syllabus and can be used as a stand-alone, or in group training settings. The course materials and coaching tools you will be provided with will quickly jumpstart your confidence in your ability to coach persons recovering from harmful addictive behaviors. You will find various coaching tools throughout that build on each other and can be put into practice the very next day following your training. All course materials are presented in practical, user friendly terms and uses easy to understand chalk-talk exercises, analogies, and metaphorical examples that can be used with clients to highlight a point or a seemingly complicated concept. Our goal is to offer training participants a unique opportunity to learn valuable skills from professionals who are using the methods daily in their work.

Training participants will be exposed to research-based, coaching paradigms that are aligned with major treatment and coaching organizations such as: ICF, CCA, NAADAC and SAMHSA which include:

✓ *How to build recovery capital.*
✓ *Incorporating Whole Life Recovery in aftercare.*
✓ *Stages of Change model.*
✓ *Coaching in multicultural settings.*
✓ *Client empowerment.*
✓ *The power of asking focused questions.*
✓ *Establishing a coaching relationship.*

✓ *Personal & professional coaching traits.*
✓ *Strengths-based coaching.*
✓ *Focused listening.*
✓ *Cognitive restructuring: challenging faulty thinking.*
✓ *Community transitional service systems.*
✓ *Laws, ethics, and boundaries.*

Bonus track:
    ✓ *Launching your own coaching enterprise.*

        ■ *Creating your vision.*
        ■ *Niche coaching.*
        ■ *Marketing techniques*
        ■ *Networking skills.*

You are what you practice

You will be seeing this ___ icon throughout the handbook. It refers to a chalk-talk exercise and asks that you push the pause button in your head and process aspects of what is being learned. It is also an effective discussion tool you can use with clients. Chalk-talk plays an important role in recovery coaching in that it is an interactive way to reflect, generate thoughts, problem-solve, and monitor what is being learned. Chalk-talk can also be used productively to maximize a coach's work by serving as a means of self-monitoring your effectiveness and progress as a coach.

There is power in chalk-talk, and when used effectively, encourages rapport and synergy and can provide clarity to the learning process. Please take the time to practice each chalk-talk exercise so that you will be better able to apply the skills you have learned.

COMPONENTS OF THE TRAINING PROGRAM

Our twenty-five hour in-person and online Recovery Coach Mastery webinar system will equip you with all the knowledge and skills needed to participate worldwide in the recovery coaching field.

What you will receive in our instructional package:

➤ Sixteen (16) hours of webinar instruction, practicum and demonstration.

➤ Four (4) hours of in-home study materials.

➤ Two (2) hours of a final mastery evaluation qualifying you as a recovery coach, and board-approved certification.

➤ Three (3) hours of follow-up consultation and Q & A's.

➤ Upon request, certified coaches will have access to our prepared, generic *"done-for-you"* coaching start-up forms, templates and other printed materials that coaches can begin using immediately.

Final Assessment

Upon completion of your training and a 75% passing score on your final mastery assessment, you will qualify for certification and be conferred the title of Professional Recovery Coach. Because of the clearly outlined materials and your practice sessions at the end of each module, you will be provided with everything needed to make your assessment experience positive and successful.

Recovery coach competencies are aligned with the professional coaching standards and principles outlined in the International Coach Federation (ICF), Recovery Coach International (RCI) and the Substance Abuse and Mental Health Services Administration (SAMSA). These organizations consider recovery as working best in community-based, holistic systems that are grounded on scientific evidence and which can document outcomes in both the clinical and real world settings. To this end, in order to demonstrate foundational knowledge of recovery coaching's core competencies, an examination for certification is necessary to give strength to the certification process and credibility to the professionals who will be providing clients with a comprehensive recovery plan.

Coach Mentoring and Assistance

We are here to help you become a successful recovery coach during and after your training. If you have any questions regarding the training you have received or need assistance regarding a coaching concern, do not hesitate to call one of our Master Coaches or send us an email. You can reach us toll free at (844) 414-8444 or email us at: info@startingpointmn.com. We will be pleased to arrange a conference call via Skype to answer any detailed questions you might have.

What you will need:

1. Our Recovery Coach Mastery handbook. It has been designed as a document to be used both as a learning and resource tool that can be referred to again and again in times of need. To find what you need, simply start at the table of contents and review each section for the needed topic. You will notice that the Table of Contents is broken up into sections or modules not chapters, listing individual skills.

2. A simple (any brand) adjustable headset with microphone.

3. Skype capability (optional).

4. A coaching buddy or volunteer (if done on-line). This will help you practice the techniques that will be presented. If you are using the handbook as a stand-alone, you will need to recruit a friend, colleague or spouse who you can rely on to serve as a real or imaginary client.

Feedback

Give and ask for feedback as much as possible. Let your master trainer know when something is not working for you or if you need help; the earlier the better. Any time you want specific or more in-depth feedback on something you are working on, please ask. Even when you have completed the program, you will have access to coaching mentors that can answer any of your questions via telephone, email or Skype technology. Recovery Coach Academy believes that direct feedback is the easiest way to ensure that you get all that you need.

Business Start-up Component

Inquiring coaches-in-training have expressed a desire to change lives in profound ways and have asked for help in expanding their current coaching role and launch their own coaching enterprise. At the very end of the handbook, Recovery Coach Academy has created a business start-up component. You will be introduced to business start-up activities and the skills needed to expand your client base. You will be provided with marketing techniques that, when done consistently, will attract clients and maintain a successful business or program.

Our business start-up component will afford you the following:

✓ *Launch a new career.*
✓ *Make yourself marketable.*
✓ *Expand your clientele base.*
✓ *Become an additional conduit for success to your clients.*
✓ *Add a new certification to your resume.*
✓ *Potential increase in your income.*

Our coaching system is becoming one of the most comprehensive in the next generation of aftercare. Our coaches are Masters Degree level and above and have invested time in developing a system that cuts to the core of a recovering individual's problems and introduce their clients to alternatives that can not only serve them well in their recovery efforts, but in life. We are proud to be in the forefront of a paradigm shift that is becoming to the 21st century, what counseling was to the 20th century.

Keep Doing What Works. Stop Doing What Doesn't.

By registering in this coaching system, you have shown a commitment to helping people extend their sobriety and fulfill their dreams. As you help facilitate change in others, don't get yourself trapped by the *"this is the way we've always done it"* thinkers. Try everything. If something in your recovery toolkit works, keep doing it. If it doesn't work, change it.

You will be ready to become that someone who will provide encouragement, and challenge your clients to achieve their greatest potential. You will become their conduit to those paths to success. Just know that from time to time those paths might change. And that is a good thing. It's called growth.

While you are with us, relax, do your best, have fun, model hope, and keep a positive attitude. You will be guiding people through some life-changing experiences, who with your help, will cause them to want to turn their lives around. Through your patience and skills, our clients will accomplish great things, and so will you. Again, we welcome you to Recovery Coaching Academy.

RECOVERY COACH CREDO

I am not a therapist. I don't treat anyone. I am a Recovery Coach. I am about growth, not rescue. My concern is about your present condition and future goals. I don't provide you with answers, but through the work we will do together, I will help and support you in your quest to find your own answers.

As your coach I will maintain a professional, but collaborative relationship that will focus on your strengths and abilities to conquer or cope with whatever is preventing you from meeting your goals or your dreams. Our relationship will be based on trust, support, experience, and mutual accountability. My goal is to help you regain or achieve a life you once dearly loved, but was lost through your addictive or compulsive behaviors. This is what I am prepared to do for you and you for yourself.

PROGRAM FOCUS

Development and growth are the aim of all we do. Recovery Coach Mastery's underlying goal is to train coaches to help and support clients in their creation of hope, confidence, and a vision for themselves.

Recovery Coach Mastery bases its training principles on scientific research. Our strengths-based system of coaching has been proven to work with a variety of addictive disorders: substance abuse, gambling, compulsions, eating disorders and codependency issues to name a few.

Even though there is a strong, generic spiritual component in a coach's repertoire, Recovery Coach Mastery does not promote any specific sequential, spiritual or psychological principle. Instead, it follows both the International Coach Federation (ICF) and Recovery Coach International (RCI) core competencies, code of ethics and best practice techniques that have been gleaned from experts in business, life coaching and the human services fields.

Growth Not Rescue

As a recovery coach, you will be about growth, not rescue. You will allow your clients the flexibility of exploring multiple paths and options while on their sober journey. Your task is to guide and support them in their selection of options and to help them devise a plan to make their chosen options a reality. Our training system emphasizes the fact that there can be several paths to sobriety and you will be helping clients explore this tenet through field-tested uses of empirical evidence, logic, and a process known as cognitive restructuring: a realignment of one's faulty thinking and beliefs.

Though our system utilizes logic and empirical evidence, you will be taught how to simplify these principles for your clients through chalk-talk discussions, the use of analogies, and Socratic or focused questioning. In doing so, you will be making seemingly complex principles less threatening and more practical for your clients to understand and apply in their own lives.

The Art of Socratic Questioning

Another role in recovery coaching is the empowerment and supporting of clients in becoming their own rescuers. Learning how to draw out a client's wisdom through questioning rather than imposing a coach's agenda, is one of the cornerstones of coaching and considered critical to a client's growth and change.

Socratic questioning, named after Socrates' style of teaching is referred to in today's circles as *Focused Questioning, Motivational* and *Intentional Interviewing and critical thinking.* No matter the term used, they all consist of three parts: 1) A discussion led by a person who does nothing but reflect and ask questions; 2) Questions are systematically phrased, sincere, disciplined and purposeful. 3) The questioner, in this case the coach, directs the discussion by the questions he/she asks and how he or she points out discrepancies in what is being said. Through focused questioning, clients are helped to go deeper beneath the surface of what is being discussed, to probe into the complexities of one or more fundamental ideas or questions. *(Rosenberg, D.B., 2012. Foundation for Critical Thinking 2006; Bannink Fredrike, 1999; Stoltzfus, T.2008).*

As a coach, you will be leading your sessions with sincere curiosity. No matter how insightful you are, the most impactful moments will be when you draw out answers from the clients themselves. There is no formula for that skill nor are there any "canned" coaching questions. What we have provided throughout this training are real questions used by coaches in their practices and you may want to memorize them, but make no mistake, the truly great coaching questions you will learn will arise through the magic of the moment. This will happen when you have coached enough sessions and when suddenly your natural curiosity will automatically lead you to a follow-up question and the next question and the next, until your client's answers lead them to that *burning bush* moment of awareness, delighting both of you. This only happens when natural curiosity is applied and the coach is fully present in the moment. You must be ready to go wherever the moment leads you or as veteran coaches say, *"Showing up for whatever shows up."* Take a few moments to check out, *Coaching Commons.org* for some super questioning materials.

Let me just reiterate two obvious axioms: 1) Nobody knows more about you than you and 2) people, as a rule, love talking about themselves. And why not? Clients are the only experts on themselves. Questioning, then, has the power to provoke people to look deeper for answers in a particular way or direction. This can often result in a quicker call to action for clients and your ability to move clients from a position of ambivalence to one of action.

As you hone your coaching skills, keep in mind that change can only be encouraged, but can never be forced, and it is not the perfect question that will cause your clients to change. So, stop seeking that Holy Grail of questions that will change a client's world. It doesn't exist. You only need to help your clients think a little farther down the road than they would have on their own. That is the magic of questioning. Just keep asking and trust the process. In time your form of questioning will build trust and empowerment. Stay relaxed, confident, and be fully present for your client. In time, change will happen.

WHAT IS RECOVERY COACHING?

"To impose one single paradigm on someone and expect them to work or live up to it is sheer madness," said the late, Albert Ellis. Recovery coaching is a person-centered, strengths-based system that upholds the notion that there can be several paths to sobriety. Recovery coaching is highly interactive in that the client is encouraged to actively participate in their own recovery. The coaching process is action oriented with an emphasis on improving present life and reaching goals for the future. It is based on the belief that people are, by their very nature, creative, resourceful and whole. They are capable of finding answers; choosing options and taking action. They are capable of recovering when things don't go as planned; and they are especially capable of learning. This capacity is hardwired into all human beings and begins with creating an initial awareness that positive change is possible, and that with guidance and support, clients can be helped to develop doable strategies that build recovery capital, and continue on toward a sustained recovery.

Recovery Coaching is about:	Recovery Coaching is **not** about:
Guiding	Therapy
Being strengths-focused	Client pathology
Communicating	Counseling
Verbalizing	Consulting
Empathetically listening	Labeling problems
Optimism	Shaming
Non-linear thinking	Linear, sequential thinking
Open acceptance of clients	Blaming
Empowering	Advising
Growth	Rescuing
Understanding of spiritual concepts	Higher Power thinking exclusively
The present-future	Excavating past traumas
Clients set the agenda	*"Do it our way,"* mentality

What is a Recovery Coach?

From time to time, everyone needs a coach: athletes, business owners, entrepreneurs, and people in transition. William White, writer on addiction treatment and policy best defined the recovery coach *as, "...A non-clinical person who helps remove internal and external obstacles to recovery, links the newly recovered person to the recovery community, and serves as a personal guide and mentor in the management of personal and family recovery. Such supports are generated through mobilizing peer-based or volunteer resources within the recovery community. Often, support may be provided by the recovery coach where such supports are lacking" (William White; 2002).*

For purposes of this training, a recovery coach is also a trained professional and an active collaborator who listens. Really listens. Listening includes non-verbal communication: listening for incongruity between what is said and not being said. When coaches listen to clients effectively, they begin to feel safe in the relationship and trust happens; often followed by change-talk.

A recovery coach is a connector of people to professionals and community resources such as housing, education, and employment, as well as community support systems and resources for shelter, food shelves, and peer recovery support organizations to name a few.

An effective recovery coach is one who encourages clients to ultimately draw their own conclusions and choose the direction they want to take in resolving their issues. There are times when a coach challenges the client to formulate a behavioral goal to address the ultimate objective and assesses how confident the client feels in achieving the particular goal.

Goals may need to be re-evaluated scaled down and gradually implement or modified altogether to optimize adherence to a plan. The coaching process then, is a collaborative, conversational style of interacting with clients in their effort move beyond their current dilemma.

EMPOWERING VISION STATEMENTS

Nothing begins without a vision. Nothing. Recovery coaching is no different. Steven Covey is credited with saying, *"The things you envision and focus on the most almost always grow."* Like plants, if you water and nurture your dreams/visions, they will grow. If you ignore them the opposite is sadly true. A compelling vision is important to recovery in that a vision can take any lost or forgotten dream and, like a weak battery, recharge it with renewed power. An important part of coaching is when a coach helps clients discover and ignite that vision in clients.

The first thing recovery coaches do in igniting that vision is to ask clients what they want out of life while in recovery; to picture in their minds what they want more of, and what it is they want less of. It could be anything from a sustained sobriety or re-building relationships. The important thing is that they must be able to visualize and articulate their dream or goal; know it, feel it, and be bold about it, almost selfish. In recovery coaching this important step is called: *Empowering Vision.* If coaches ignore this important step, recovering clients run the risk of their dreams never being truly fulfilled.

Many recovering persons are not really certain about who they are anymore and what they really want to do with their lives after an addiction. They lack an understanding of how one can now live life purposefully or if pursuing one's dream is even a possibility. For some, clues to a better life are already beginning to show, but to many others, life in recovery is still a blind spot. They express fear and doubt about their ability to recover from past behaviors and express uncertainty about this whole coaching experience. They go through life feeding themselves negative self-talk and incessantly focus on what they *can't* do; putting themselves down as a result of shame and self-loathing. Yet, when you probe the surface, they all have an *inner knowing*; a dream, and a yearning for something better. *(For greater detail on visualization exercises check out Terri Cole at www.terricole.com.)*

Look into →

Fears to consider when opening up in writing

Fear can be a very common by-product of recovery. There is the fear of being alone, of change, failure or of making mistakes. Finally, there is the failure of not having what it takes to reach our goals and relapsing. These are all common fears experienced by persons in recovery and as a client once expressed to me, *"You know how easy it is for us to screw up a good thing."*

Recovery coaches work at helping clients identify and challenge any potential fears that may still be lingering in recovery. Coaches teach clients that obstacles can have power over us if we let them remain covered up in the depths of our minds and are not brought out into the light. Journaling or writing out one's vision of a doable future; of what CAN be, is one way of confronting our fears.

Empowering Vision Statements (EVS)

There is an old quote: *"If you don't know what you want, you'll end up with what you get."* Many recovering clients seek recovery coaching not really knowing what it is that they want out of life, beyond staying sober, and are looking for a catch-all or quick-fix tool *(a DVD, a workbook, etc),* that can help them but that doesn't always work.

A good empowerment visioning works best in helping clients prepare grasp a better picture of what they could become or what their dream will look like down the road as they grow during their sober journey. An Empowering Vision Statement (EVS) is a good way of getting deep in the weeds and focusing on attaining better clarity of what is meant by an *achievable* and *sober* future:

✓ *What is your life about now that you're in recovery?*

✓ *What do you stand for?*

✓ *What do you value?*

✓ *What are you good at?*

✓ *What kinds of activities, roles or responsibilities energize you?*

✓ *What sucks your energies dry?*

✓ *What actions do you take to manifest your purpose and your values?*

✓ *What are things you've wanted to do, but were temporarily detoured by addiction?*

✓ *What experiences in life have you had that gave you a sudden and unusual sense of purpose?*

✓ *How would a good friend describe you what you are like today?*

✓ *What have your life experiences told you about your destiny? How accurate are they and can they be changed?*

✓ *What sense of purpose have you drawn from your family, culture or community?*

✓ *Name three things that would definitely be a part of your change process.*

Vision Has Power

Visioning exercises provide clients with inspiration, a sense of direction and clarity, so they can go through their days knowing clearly what their dream (or goal) can look like once it has been accomplished.

All the more reason for an EVS to be inspirational. If what clients write is flat or boring, they are probably not going to want to do anything about taking action and moving forward with their lives. A life vision has power and should be aligned with new values, and be inspiring so that clients want to take action towards it.

23

MMFI Rule

All coaches should strive to instill inspiration and motivation in their clients. Coaches cannot be at their highest level of service to others if they are not making their clients feel important and valued. One way to do this is to implement my MMFI rule. I use MMFI with everyone I meet, but especially in the first days of our coaching sessions. MMFI is the acronym for Make Me Feel Important.

Imagine every person you encounter has the letters MMFI hanging around their neck. How much better would this world be? Better yet, why can't we make all potential clients we meet, feel important? Try it the next chance you get and you will see the changes it makes on others...and you. Not only will you succeed in recovery coaching, you will succeed in life.

Try this exercise:

Using small Post-it notes write the letters MMFI and ask each one of your participants to place the note on their foreheads where everyone can see it. Then assign a 15 minute time period to have them meander around the room talking to each other about a specific topic of your choosing. Example:

What do you value in life?
What will your life look like three months in the future?

Bring the group together and discuss each others' listening skills as it relates to making the other party feel important...valued.

Developing an Empowering Vision Statement

Visioning is astonishingly powerful for two reasons. First, when clients allow themselves to envision a doable future, they are sweeping off the table all limited considerations. At first, clients will tend to become surprised by what they have written. And second, having seen the wonderful things that could lie ahead, they will become motivated and empowered to explore an array of opportunities, make decisions, and venture forth in a much clearer and purposeful way. Visioning generates hope, encouragement and offers a possibility for fundamental change. It gives people a sense of control and something to move toward.

What EVS accomplishes:

- Strengthens client commitment.
- Generates creative thinking and passion.
- It helps clients develop consistency and follow-through.
- Provides on-going feedback and support.
- Fosters client self-confidence.
- Celebrates results.

Below are some strength-focused tips you can use to help recovering clients develop their EVS. With your coaching partner, begin to role play the visioning exercise below by asking each other the questions which have been provided:

Visioning Prompts

 Setting the stage:
1. "Imagine that a miracle happened overnight and your goal had been met, however you were asleep and unaware the miracle happened. What would you see different about your situation? Let's write it down."
2. "Close your eyes and envision twelve months into the future as your goal is being met. What will the accomplished goal look like?"
3. "How important is your goal to your well-being?"

4. "How much (or whom) are you willing to sacrifice to make sobriety (or goal) your priority?"
5. "Identify barriers: internal, external, or karmatic." *(It wasn't meant to be.)*
6. "Are there support systems/personal/internal/external that can help you meet your goal?"
7. "How does your goal guide your decisions to proceed?"
8. "When will you start? By when will you reach your goal?"
9. "Who will you celebrate meeting your goal with?"

Strength-Focused Questioning used in EVS:

For centuries, philosophers have always taught that the wise man is not the one who provides the right answers, but the one who asks the right questions. This is especially true in recovery coaching. Focused questioning is used when clients are stuck in a place or are unclear on what to say or do next. The best possible thing a coach can do in these situations is to help clients find words for the intuitive feel of the present issue through questioning. Once the client is helped to express in words what is going on inside them, solutions and next steps will come more easily. Begin by holding a discussion around the following strength-focused questions:

1. "Recall a time in your life when you were doing well. What was different then? How can it be different now?"
2. "What were you doing then, that you could do now?"
3. "What are you really great at?"
4. "What are your best talents or natural abilities?"
5. "What are five of your key strengths (list them)?"
6. "What are some (sober) accomplishments you have made that should be celebrated?"
7. "Talk about a challenge you overcame without (*add habit*)."
8. "When do you feel most proud of yourself?"
9. "What positive things do people say about you?"
10. "How did you manage to overcome the challenges you have faced?"

This is a good time to be supportive, enthusiastic, and positive. Nurture your clients' strengths as they begin to create those small steps that can empower them to take bigger ones. In time, those small steps will become huge leaps and bounds.

Building Inspiration to Write

When we set a goal, there is the tendency to forget it or put it on the back burner. An EVS can help remind and guide us towards achieving our goals. An EVS gives us the perception of a successful future and helps us stay focused on which direction to proceed in achieving our goals. It motivates and drives us to experience an advance sense of satisfaction upon finally having or becoming what we so badly want to have or be.

EVS Instructions to recovering clients

Writing an Empowering Vision Statement will be one of the most powerful and significant activities you will ever do to re-take control of your life. Your EVS will help you identify the most important roles, relationships, and things in your life. Your EVS will reveal who you want to be, what you want to do, who you want to do it with, and the legacy you want to leave to others. This is how you can do it:

1. Write your goal over and over again until you achieve the feel that best describes what you want to have, be, or experience.
2. Begin listing those things that evoke the right emotion and drive in you.
3. Write down the things that inspire you and that makes you want to make a commit to and work hard at.
4. Write the things you're already good at so that you can reinforce your faith in yourself.
5. Write your EVS as if you have already achieved what you desire...your dream.
6. Use power words that influence and motivate you to want to meet your goal.

A client's EVS can be as short or as long as clients want it to be. However, it should explicitly state what they want and have set out to achieve and written in a manner that shows that the client has already achieved it. It is these types of written affirmations that almost always lead to exploring options and taking action.

Power words and phrases which can be used when writing an EVS:

- ✓ Accomplishing
- ✓ Enjoying
- ✓ Expanding
- ✓ Flourishing
- ✓ Becoming
- ✓ Exceeding
- ✓ Thriving
- ✓ Transforming

- ✓ Results
- ✓ Harmonious
- ✓ Can
- ✓ Discovering
- ✓ Inspired
- ✓ Realizing
- ✓ Possibilities
- ✓ Transitioning

Toxic words and phrases that can kill motivation:

- Yes, but…
- I don't think so
- If only…
- Try
- Someday

- Maybe
- Might
- Should have
- Could have
- Wasn't meant to be

Questioning Strategies when writing an EVS

- Always ask the miracle question first: *"Suppose one night, while you are asleep, a miracle happened and are now living your future, what does that look like?...Now write it down."*
- Follow up with a series of leading questions: *"What would be different? Have there been times when you have seen pieces of this miracle happen? Under what conditions? What's the first step that you can take to begin making this miracle happen? Good, now write it down."*
- Practice the pregnant pause. It is never a good idea to force anyone to comment or respond. Sometimes it is best to pause and wait the client out.
- Give feedback, not advice. Use the process of paraphrasing. It is more powerful to help clients find their own words for the experience they are having: *"What could be a better way of expressing that?"*

Examples of Empowerment Vision Statements

Example 1 (Weight loss; written one year in advance)
I have shed 15 pounds, and I look marvelous. I'm sitting in a lounge chair on the beach in Cabo and I sense that everyone is checking me out. My husband has begun a renewed interest in me and our relationship is flourishing. I have never felt happier or healthier than I do today. My weight loss has made me more confident and I am discovering things about me that before my weight loss were impossible and have transformed myself into a marathon runner and am making plans to complete my college education. I have begun to realize my career potential and am one of two finalists in a job interview. I'm one step closer to my dream job.

Example 3 (Aftercare treatment; written one year in advance)

I have finally quit drinking and smoking. I've successfully completed a recovery coaching program and have a clearer vision of what I want to do with the rest of my life. I am beginning to feel like I do have a second chance at fulfilling my dream of finishing school and through my coach's help have begun to embrace a life that was once fragmented and is now filled with possibilities. I got my old job back, I jog every morning and am taking the positives steps to get my wife and family back. The flourishing youth leadership position that I have volunteered for has me seeing the great results in transforming lives while giving me personal side benefits and joy. I am discovering that life itself is what now gives me a natural high, and I no longer need chemicals to make me feel fulfilled.

CHALK TALK

EVS Writing (exercise)

Write your own Empowering Vision Statement regarding your becoming a masterful recovery coach. Write it as if you are looking ahead five years and your coaching business is bearing fruit. Don't forget to use the power phrases listed above.

Writing prompt:

As I sit in my office enjoying the quiet sounds of my stereo playing. I envision..._____

_____

_____

_____

_____

_____

_____

_____

_____

_____

_____

_____

_____

_____

_____

_____

_____

_____

_____

_____

_____

NOTES

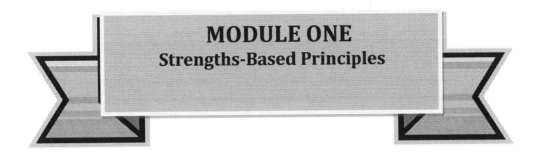

MODULE ONE
Strengths-Based Principles

This module will enable coaches to:

- ➢ Define the guiding principles of *strengths-based recovery.*
- ➢ Explore the history, characteristics and function of Recovery Coaching.
- ➢ Examine concept of recovery.
- ➢ Explore key elements of *recovery capital.*
- ➢ Gain knowledge of the coaching process.
- ➢ Identify recovery coach competencies.

PARADIGM SHIFT IN AFTERCARE

To quote an old Bob Dylan tune, *"The times they are a-changing..."* Guess what? The times have already changed. Stop using "old School" solutions that may no longer work to resolve modern-day problems. Treatment and aftercare modalities have drastically changed. Today, we are dealing with a 21st century, drug and alcohol using population that finds itself in different cognitive and psychic places: *Millennials (born between 1981-1995)* and *Gen Xers (born between 1961-1980).* Both are a more complex group of human beings than our previous 20th century clients.

Millennials are said to be narcissistic, highly empowered by technology and their electronic devices have become extensions of their bodies. Millennials also have a strong sense of entitlement and believe that consequences can be easily negotiated or are immune to consequences altogether. Millennials are more into *hooking up* than dating and gender equality is a given.

Their drug of choice is said to be pot, prescription drugs and anything else that gives them immediate gratification. If addicted, millennials will not seek treatment (*that's old school*) unless a catastrophic event occurs such as a near death experience, jail, a court mandate, an auto accident, or serious law enforcement involvement and then...maybe. This may be because consequences have not been serious enough for this group or that the parental protection they have received has kept them insulated from consequences.

Gen Xers, on the other hand are now parents or single adults. They tend to be more entrepreneurial, better E-networkers and seem preoccupied in dealing with pressures about the future. They have grown up during the Internet revolution and are technology adapters. Generally, the drug most abused is pot and cocaine for men, and alcohol and Adderall for women. What makes Adderall attractive to women and the prime motive for abuse is that it helps them multi-task (*superwomen, supermoms*) and lose weight at the same time.

It's a family affair

Now, this has not been a attempt to paint all millennials and Gen Xers as wrong and hopeless. Many have their heads on straight, and good for them. The only point being made here is that from these two groups come parents, though not addicts who have smoked pot and chemically indulged in their younger days and today have an open attitude about alcohol and drugs, especially in light of the current legalization trend of marijuana in this nation. It comes as no surprise then that everything is now out in the open. Nothing is really forbidden.

Old school models vs. new-age clients

In their adjustment to a rapidly changing complex world both generations seem to be dealing with greater stressors than their baby boomer predecessors. Point being, traditional models of the past (snazzy slides, shame and blame programs and activities for example)   may not be as effective for this population.

As a result of this sudden demographic paradigm shift in using behaviors, we are seeing a population that responds best to models that are based on common-sense principles which are practical, life-affirming and help hold themselves accountable. They don't need to be told that they are crazy or immoral as they may have been told that already.

Those who have made a commitment to remain sober may be too busy to sit in a circle admitting defeat to strangers while others avoid the stigma *(I'm in treatment)* associated with quasi-religious paradigms. They already know they are drug or alcohol dependent and are ready to explore practical solutions *(I'm doin' a little life coaching)* that can get their lives back on track as quickly as possible. They are living in fear of reusing, but they can't seem to find the proper tools needed to maintain their sobriety. That's where recovery coaching can help.

STRENGTHS-BASED PRINCIPLES

Because recovery coaching can be deeply personal, it needs to be a highly recovery-oriented, community-based and client-centered system of aftercare. Individual empowerment is an essential ingredient of recovery along with community reintegration and normalization of a client's life environment *(SAMHSA, 2008)*. To this end, developing clients' strengths and encouraging their aspirations can lead to the building of recovery capital, personal growth and accomplishments after treatment. Building recovery capital is a major cornerstone of recovery.

What is Strengths-based Recovery Coaching?

Supporting clients in their innate abilities to recover from any addictive disorder is a cornerstone of recovery coaching. The strengths-based paradigm emphasizes a person's self-determination, commitment, inherent strengths and self-accountability, while applying them to present and future outcomes. Recovery coaching, then, has to be highly interactive and client led in that clients are encouraged to define their own life goals supported in the design of a unique path or plan towards those goals. The model is based on two principles:

1) Every client has unique, individual strengths, abilities and assets that can be used in their recovery process. It does not take a psychoanalytical or spiritual approach exclusively to help clients. The approach is of the belief that every client, given the proper support,

mutual trust and training, has the inner capacity and power to maintain his or her sobriety.

2) Clients become participants in their own recovery when they are given the tools needed to challenge their thinking errors and beliefs, develop their own personalized paths or action plans, and seek out the appropriate resources in their community that can move their recovery in a forward motion.

(Sources: NIDA-Cognitive Behavioral Approach (2009) ; William Miller and Stephen Rollnick. (2002).

To recap, the coach and client work in collaboration to make these two principles happen, but it is the client who chooses which strengths or resources to tap into or reject. The coach's objectives are to serve as support and accountability partner using a process of focused questioning or intentional inquiry *("...and how will that option work for you?")*, and guiding and helping clients identify and achieve goals they have chosen for themselves.

Strengths-based recovery coaching is:

- Action oriented with a focus on the present and the future.
- Short-term, but critically important during the first twelve months of recovery. It works best when there is a strong desire to willingly work towards a sober lifestyle.
- Based on collaboration rather than a top-down relationship.
- Transitional and goal-oriented: "Where are you now and where do you wish to be tomorrow?" It works when clients take control of and responsibility for their future.
- Solution-focused. Helps clients become their own rescuers.
- Practical and non-clinical. Does not focus on past traumas.
- Accepting of clients' present situation.
- Educational and interactive. Teaches clients how to question their own faulty thinking patterns, to self-counsel, and to implement a doable/realistic plan.

It is not recovery coaching if a coach:

- Argues that the client has a problem and needs to change.

- Offers direct advice or prescribes solutions to the problem without the client's permission or without actively encouraging the client to make his or her own choices.
- Uses an authoritative/expert stance leaving the client in a passive role.
- Does most of the talking, or functions as a unidirectional information delivery system.
- Imposes a diagnostic label to a problem.
- Behaves in a punitive or coercive manner.

What is Recovery?

Alcoholism and addiction are problems that defy easy solutions. The principles of a sound recovery model have been delineated by SAMHSA, a public health agency within the U.S. Department of Health and Human Services and provide us with a sample of some common elements of recovery and the building or rebuilding of recovery capital:

- ✓ **Recovery emerges from hope:** *The belief that recovery is real and provides the essential and motivating message of a better future. People can and do overcome the internal and external challenges, barriers, and obstacles that confront them.*

- ✓ **Recovery is person-driven**: *Self-determination and self-direction are the foundations for recovery as individuals define their own life goals and design their unique path(s).*

- ✓ **Recovery occurs via many pathways:** *Individuals are unique with distinct needs, strengths, preferences, goals, culture, and backgrounds that affect and determine their pathway(s) to recovery.*

- ✓ **Recovery is holistic:** *Recovery encompasses an individual's whole life including mind, body, spirit, and community. The array of services and supports available should be integrated and coordinated.*

- ✓ **Recovery is supported by peers and allies**: *Mutual support and mutual aid groups, including the sharing of experiential knowledge and skills, as we as social learners all play an invaluable role in recovery. (For further detailed information on these and other principles visit: http://www.samhsa.gov/recovery/.)*

What is Recovery Capital?

Aftercare researchers Robert Granfield and William Cloud in their book, *Coming Clean: Overcoming Addiction without Treatment* defined recovery capital as:

"... the breadth and depth of internal and external resources that can be drawn upon to initiate and sustain recovery from severe [addictions]. (Granfield & Cloud, 1999; Cloud & Granfield, 2004.)."

From this definition, one can conclude that recovery coaching is about helping and supporting clients build and maintain a healthy supply of emotional, social, environmental, and spiritual capital in one's recovery account. The intent being that when confronted with challenges, clients are better able to spend down on some of that capital in combatting barriers that may pop up in their efforts to maintain and sustain long-term sobriety.

Types of Recovery Capital

The types of recovery capital are outlined in Whole Life Recovery of module two and include:

➤ Physical capital: health, employment, financial assets.
➤ Intellectual capital: recovery skills, knowledge.
➤ Emotional capital: values, commitment, goodwill, love of self and others.
➤ Social capital: supportive relationships, resources, culture.
➤ Spiritual capital: guiding principles, moral compass, a purpose in life, and a spiritual centeredness.

What do you get back in recovery? One's *self!* How much recovery capital a person has can almost always determine how easy or how hard of a time they will have in getting themselves on the difficult journey to sobriety. This does not mean that someone who has less recovery capital can't get sober, it just means they will have to build more of it over time in order to maintain their sobriety. Given the right tools, most people in their sober journey can build recovery capital whether they begin with none at all or only a little. It is possible for everyone to have enough capital in their account to begin their recovery journey and through solid maintenance, remain or extend their sobriety.

First Steps

Below are some very basic first steps that master coaches recommend clients do from the onset:

- Attend outpatient recovery coaching or concurrently participate in some form of aftercare.
- Begin building relationships with others committed to sobriety.
- Attend peer-based sobriety support meetings (AA, NA, etc.)
- Have a solid relapse plan in place.
- Obtain employment or further your education.
- Pay forward your good fortune by volunteering in community projects.
- Strengthen you spiritual centeredness by praying, meditating or reading materials that provide hope and strength.
- Participate in programs that are spiritually uplifting.
- Learn to have fun again while living sober.

The Coach as Accountability Partner

As a final point, recovery coaches also serve as *accountability partners*. They teach clients new ways to live and how to follow through on their plans regardless of the obstacles before them. Coaches provide opportunities for clients to learn self-accountability, which in turn fuels their strength and hope, throughout the coach-client relationship.

In short, a recovery coach provides support, motivation, and accountability by:

- ✓ Encouraging clients to explore options and solutions.

- ✓ Teaching and supporting clients on how to set and devise a plan for reaching their goals.
- ✓ Encouraging clients to ask more of themselves and to reach higher.
- ✓ Providing structure and accountability.
- ✓ Helping clients challenge their erroneous thinking.
- ✓ Helping clients draw distinctions, and offering perspectives.
- ✓ Helping clients see (and believe) that there is hope and life after addiction.

As we have illustrated, the recovery coach is an authentic professional who teaches clients that there are several paths to their goal. Coaches also understand that paths often change over time, and that might very well be a good thing. We call it *growth*, and isn't that the goal of recovery coaching?

"We are products of our past, but we don't have to be prisoners of it."

(Rick Warren)

BARRIERS AND OTHER CHALLENGES TO RECOVERY

The First Ninety Days

Quitting is an important event or process, but it is not necessarily recovery. Aftercare in the first year of recovery is vital with the first ninety days being the most critical. Few people know that the notion to relapse begins in the mind and how internal dialog can play havoc in people's minds as they struggle with the challenges of recovery. Clients who come to coaching are often seemingly confused and perpetually angry. It is because during this period two major barriers to maintaining sobriety are getting in the way of their recovery: *internal* (self-loathing, shame and self-doubt) and *external*; missing links or resources that can ensure transitional success (sober and age-appropriate support groups, employment, housing needs).

There are two things in life that can quickly create sweaty palms: *commitment* and *change*. Change is a scary thing to recovering individuals, indeed, to all of us. Compound that fear and anxiety with the fact that in the initial stages of abstinence, recovering individuals must begin to examine an array of options, one of which is having to consider making major physical and social lifestyle changes all at once.

Social scientists correctly assert that when society or persons labels individuals, they become that label. But when individuals cognitively re-label or redefine themselves, change happens. That in a nutshell is the process of recovery coaching: supporting clients in redefining themselves and their situation.

Clients in recovery may not have the confidence or skills to fully understand and manage their lives at first. They are faced with the pressures of having to deal with transitional fears and distorted beliefs that might not have been fully addressed in treatment and are still in need of a period of restructuring. Treatment professionals call this *residual cognitive dissonance.* Recovery coaches call it *addictive thinking.* The AA folks simply call it *stinky thinking.* There are several reasons for these terms. Remember that treatment facilities as a rule only have a maximum of 28 days with a client, seven of which may be devoted to stabilization and orientation. Because a treatment facility operates on its own (insurance-driven) agenda and not the client's, this small treatment window does not allow time for in-depth restructuring of clients' thinking habits (often referred to as a treatment "add-on"). Couple that with AA being viewed as too linear and inflexible, it comes as no surprise that recovery coaching is becoming a popular and important component of continued aftercare.

Barriers or obstacles are anything internal or external that prevents a client from getting from point **A** to Point **B.** In recovery coaching terms, point *A* is where the client is at currently in his or her recovery journey. Point *B* is the dream, the goal or the point where the client wants to be in terms of recovery and life goals. Point *B* is measured in terms of days, weeks, or years. The role of recovery coaches is to teach and coach their clients on how to move forward in meeting those goals.

Internal Barriers

This bears repeating: the first internal barrier in aftercare recovery is the *shame* and *fear* that is felt by being regarded as a moral failure by self and others and the fear of not being able to overcome it. The effects of shame often may still lie below the surface of various addictive habits. Unless coaches help the recovering individual address that shame and fear through a process of identifying and confronting those fears, a true recovery can be very difficult to achieve.

Internal barriers also manifest themselves in the areas of the emotional, mental, spiritual (unable to live a purposeful life), or karmatic challenges (*maybe it wasn't meant to be*). But the most common one is self-doubt; a belief that one does not deserve anything good or decent. Many recovering clients have lost their balance in life and don't know where to turn or if they can ever begin again. The immediate response to their imbalance is one of profound shame and self-loathing to the point many become driven to revisit old addictive patterns: denial, dishonesty, isolation, and blaming exterior circumstances. Some may feel there is no solid basis for staying sober so they revert to drinking and drugging; old habits, though dangerous, have in the past been as natural and necessary as breathing.

External Barriers

An *external* barrier could be anything from housing needs, child care, employment, transportation, lack of a link to community and governmental resources that can improve a client's current condition and help him or her transition successfully. In recovery coaching, the community is viewed as a cafeteria of options where the coach helps clients select from a wide range of options that are available in their recovery efforts. The recovery coach also recognizes the importance of E-resources and utilizes those on a client's behalf.

The first and most important step to overcoming barriers in recovery is to create a more balanced life for ourselves through the participation in programs that build recovery capital in key life domains. At Starting Point we find it convenient to divide our lives into five parts which we call *life domains* so as to better teach clients that we all have critical life domains that must be kept in balance in order to maintain our sobriety and promote a healthier lifestyle. This is helpful in talking about one part of life at a time. We have named this principle *Whole Life Recovery.*

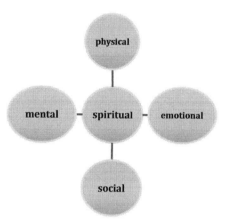

Higher levels of recovery capital = Higher quality of life.

WHOLE LIFE RECOVERY: A Master Plan for Life

The late Earnie Larsen suggested that the first stage of addiction recovery is *saving one's life*. The second stage is *rebuilding it*. Recovery then, is more than just staying away from addictive behaviors. What Larsen maintained was that a person's recovery can be greatly enhanced by rebuilding the life that was saved, and through the process of rebuilding one's life, a person could get better than just *well*.

What Earnie Larsen was alluding to and is being incorporated in recovery coaching is the concept of building recovery capital through a holistic paradigm we call *Whole Life Recovery* which encompasses five determinants in maintaining long-time sobriety in clients. The paradigm consists of five life domains that recovering individuals must keep in balance throughout their recovery journey and life: the *physical, emotional, mental, social* and *spiritual*.

What is Whole Life Recovery?

Successful recovery coaching incorporates Whole Life Recovery in its work with recovering clients in an effort to make the point that change is non-linear and may come from any direction of life's five domains which, as previously stated, include: the *physical, mental, emotional social and spiritual* domains. Eastern and Western traditions have been emphasizing, that everyone has five life aspects of wellness or domains which are critical for maintaining a healthy and balanced life and which are now becoming key to recovery from substances and other addictive disorders. In recovery, clients are encouraged to explore ways of creating change by building and maintaining recovery capital in these five domains.

46

Whole Life Recovery coaching is about helping people create healthier lifestyles for themselves. In Whole Life Recovery, life is about moving forward and being in constant change. When relating this concept to addictive and compulsive behaviors, the recovering individual is said to also be in a state of change; ever evolving from a state of active and harmful disorders for example, to a state of physical, mental, emotional, social and spiritual wellness.

Whole Life Recovery takes from Buddhist teachings that suggests we are all a part of one natural system and that an individual's life is whole when one's life domains are in harmony with that system. It is through these five life domains working together to revitalize and balance our bodies, minds and spirit, that we become *whole*. Stay with me. This is not new-age hocus pocus. This philosophy has a critical impact on one's ability to recover from any addictive behavior and is (or should be) the spirit and foundation in our quest in promoting peace, tranquility, and happiness in our, and a recovering person's life.

How Does Whole Life Recovery Work?

Imagine for a moment that our body is like an automobile with four tires, and a steering wheel. The tires and the steering wheel represent five life domains needed to guide us along life's journey, in this case, sobriety.

Physical   **Mental**   **Emotional**   **Social**   **Spiritual**

Just like in an automobile, in order to ensure a safe journey we must keep our tires balanced and our hands on the wheel at all times. There will be times when we need to identify how one or several life domains are affecting our recovery so that we can give each special attention. Breaking problems down into life domains in recovery helps us identify where we need the most help and isolates problem-solving challenges more easily. Our task then is to heal, develop, nurture by keeping all life domains in balance.

Recovery then is not just about staying away addictive behaviors. It is about building up recovery capital in all five life domains and maintaining the strength to keep them in balance as one makes positive lifestyle changes. I'm not real good with analogies, but I have found them useful when explaining concepts that may seem murky to understand. A good example is how I use the automobile analogy to explain the Whole life Recovery concept to our clients. Try it and see if it works for you.

BUILDING RECOVERY CAPITAL IN LIFE'S FIVE DOMAINS

A successful businessman and coaching client once commented, *"No matter how far down the road we've traveled, we're all the same distance from some ditch. None of us is exempt."*

Having surveyed the various life domains presented above, it is hopefully clearer to you which domain (or domains) of your life have been depleted of its recovery capital and as a result is causing us problems that will push us in a ditch at any point along our sober journey. Whether in recovery or not, keep in mind that from time to time we all may be dealing with complex, complicated problems often in more than one aspect or domain of our lives. Knowing what parts of our lives is being affected by problems helps point points us towards a better understanding of the nature of those problems. However, knowing what hurts is not quite the same thing as knowing what is causing the hurt in the first place. So we must use what we have learned about Whole Life Recovery and apply it to the world in which we interact in a manner that we can come up with explanations of what is wrong with what we are doing or not doing to maintain ourselves in balance. Let's study each of life's domains individually and assess where we are with each and what needs doing to maintain a balance.

Balance is the Challenge

Physical domain refers to the physical body (brain included); the biological aspect of addiction and possibly addiction's first casualty. When addiction becomes the focus of one's life, hygiene may suffer, and one's life becomes dominated by triggers and cravings. As the immune system becomes compromised, some people experience near-death experiences while others actually die.

Our task as recovery coaches then, is to guide and support our clients through a process of exploring ways to begin building recovery capital by reconnecting with the physical element; taking back good health and maintaining stability through physical care. Physical exercise is important to recovery, and those who get in the habit of exercising report that it energizes them in ways they never could have predicted. For some people, exercise has certain spiritual qualities that seem to enhance other areas of their lives such as greater emotional balance and mental growth.

Mental or cognitive domain is comprised of our ability to think and reason, and consists of our thoughts, beliefs, and values. It is the foundation with which recovery coaching is built. In living a drug-induced lifestyle, the addicted mind became hijacked by drugs of choice which distorted the users' thinking capabilities. You could say that their recovery capital became depleted to the point that they were kept in a perpetual state of confusion. Their thinking became irrational and choices became limited. Couple this with values being out of sync with reality, and one can see the horrendous personal, spiritual, social and legal problems that addiction can cause.

Through recovery coaching, clients are taught numerous ways of building recovery capital. One way is by challenging their distorted thinking patterns and beliefs, and to make continuous reality checks. As minds become clearer, clients become stronger and can better understand that their former addiction cannot define who they are as individuals and that each has the inner capacity to adopt new and healthier ways of looking at the world.

Emotional domain is about feeling and experiencing life in deep ways. It is the part of us that seeks meaningful contact with others. In living a drug-induced lifestyle, the recovering individual gave up on or avoided all contact with those he valued and loved. Waking hours were spent courting the obsession most loved: addictive behaviors. The truth became blurred or lost as lies and false justifications were made. Addiction requires some form of deception. You have to lie just to maintain your addiction. The slippery slope to relapse always seems to begin with some form of dishonesty and self-deception. Fresh out of treatment, many recovering clients have no means or direction as to how to forgive themselves and pursue the forgiveness of those they have harmed while *living the life*.

In order to make progress in recovery, one needs to have what recovery coaches refer to as, *"a transformation of character; an attitude adjustment."* As our values and attitudes change, we change; and by changing, we build up recovery capital that strengthens and transforms us. As we become better able to confront the man (or woman) in the mirror, we begin to forgive ourselves and begin asking those we hurt for forgiveness.

Social domain consists of activities that promote wellness within the client's circle: family, career, and financial. People are social creatures who usually need the comfort and support of healthy relationships with other people before they can feel truly good about themselves. When we began getting caught up in addictive behaviors, we became part of an addictive or using culture that had as its foundation *shared addictive values.*

Recovery then, is about moving into a new mental state; a new neighborhood and relationships that now have in it a culture of newly shared values; values that are now positive and support sobriety and enhances well-being. It is about building caring relationships with others and engaging in activities that promote social capital. The social element also has a career and financial component that is not often considered. Career, meaningful work, and financial security are pillars to a sustained recovery and impact all areas in our social lives. It is what one taps into in times of emergencies.

When recovery capital has been depleted in the other four life domains, being financially sound becomes important when trying to shore up those life domains needing attention such as joining a gym, social and recreational activities, or attending some sort of spiritual retreat. Though there are many things that recovery persons can do that don't cost money, some form of financial stability still plays an important role in maintaining one's sobriety.

Spiritual domain is one's steering wheel and resides in the center of our soul. It is what steers us in the right direction much like our moral compass. It is (or should be) a part of who we are. It is that place that extends beyond time and space; the *"who am I and why am I here?"* part of life. It is not necessarily a religion, but it can be. Basically, it is a spiritual centeredness within us that says that we are a small part of something greater than us; that we belong. While living the drug-induced lifestyle, addicted persons become disconnected from their spiritual entity and soon lose their purpose in life. The A.A. folks refer to it as being *spiritually bankrupt*; a loss of connection to one's Higher Power. Spiritually bankrupt people have, in essence, lost their moral compass, and as a result of their poor choices soon veer off the path and wind up that proverbial ditch previously spoke of.

Through building recovery capital in the spiritual domain, clients can be taught to risk a little and discover their inner path and become encouraged to try performing little acts of kindness and have it be alright because the response from those acts alone makes one feel good internally. For many, spirituality provides hope, a source of support, comfort during difficult times, and a sense of peace and understanding. It is discovering the power of being spiritually grounded that can change isolation and self-pity into a newfound peace.

The spiritual domain is about regaining or rebuilding our moral character through the practice of humility, tolerance, forgiveness, responsibility, harmony, and concern for others. Persons who have incorporated spirituality in their sober journey, have been found to recover from their addictive disorders faster and seem to maintain their sobriety for longer periods.

Reconnection is the Solution

So, if disconnection from any or all five life domains and a loss of purpose was a problem while addicted, then shouldn't *reconnection* be the solution? Whole Life Recovery encourages clients to see life a bit clearer and set priorities for addressing each life domain. Life can make sense once again, but only through the exploration of purpose-driven choices and strive to not only regain what was lost through addiction, but to exceed that. In recovery, indeed throughout our days on this planet, we must discover the joy that a balanced life can bring, and begin to discover that we are capable of, and truly deserving of a happy life. And isn't that the essence of recovery?

 **Replenishing Recovery Capital**

Begin the healing. (Use your personal situation or role play a client.) Where have you depleted your recovery capital? Rate your satisfaction with each of the five life domains below on a scale from 1-10 (10 being best/highest). What stands out to you as you look at the rankings of each life element? Talk about your highest and lowest scores. Which life element(s) are you most motivated to work on?

Physical	Mental	Emotional	Social	Spiritual

Rate ____   ____   ____   ____   ____

What do you think you ought to do to in each domain to replenish your recovery capital?

Physical well-being:

_____

_____

Mental well- being:

_____

_____

Emotional well-being:

_____

_____

Social well-being:

_____

_____

Social well-being subcategories:

    a. Education_____

        _____

    b. Career_____

        _____

    c. Financial well-being

        _____

        _____

    d. Relationship(s)

        _____

        _____

    e. Overall self-esteem

        _____

        _____

Spiritual well-being:

_____

_____

➢ What are some life goals and dreams that you want to accomplish in life?

    _____

    _____

➢ Name three steps you can begin taking today to get to where you want to be.

    _____

    _____

➢ Name 3 key people that help and support you in getting where you want to be.

    _____

    _____

➢ Now that you're in recovery, which of the 5 life areas do you wish to focus your energies on?

    _____

    _____

THE COACHING PROCESS

Recovery coaching is also about helping clients in transition envison and create the type of life they deserve, thus making the physical, social and financial investment they have made in staying sober worthwhile. Recovery coaches believe that everyone has a right to be happy and that people are not powerless, but have the strength within to maintain long-term sobriety. The Empowering Vision Statement exercise is the portal by which recovering clients begin their journey.

There are a variety of techniques used by recovery coaches to get clients through their first ninety days and beyond which you'll learn in subsequent modules. But for now, it is important to understand the basic coaching process or what experts of the Motivational Interviewing movement refer to as OARS, an acronym for four basic client-centered communication skills used in coaching: *Open question*, *Afirmation*, *Relection*, and *Summary*. Within the OARS acronym reside eight techniques that represent the main characteristics of recovery coaching. *(W. Miller S. Rollnick, 1993)*. They include:

Clarifying client needs: This is really important. People often begin a coaching session by describing what's only feasible within what they perceive as their limited skills, strengths and options. Seldom do they begin with what they really want or need or what is possible to achieve. We call this self-limiting thinking and rob clients' of the opportunity to begin thinking and setting creative goals that can truly motivate them. To prevent this from happening, coaches ask clients what they would like each session to focus on or to imagine what they want their next six months to look like, for example.

This empowers the client from the start to become active and purposeful in their coaching.

Instilling motivation and commitment: This is where the coach supports the client in finding different ways of expression and exploring options which can smooth out their coaching sessions. A master coach does this through a process of unconditional acceptance of the client's current situation (absolute worth/valuing). It includes giving affirmations, reframing comments and questions, supporting client autonomy, and providing clients with personal feedback.

Assessing a client's current status: Coaching is about helping clients get from point A to point B. Once clients express their needs, the coach helps and supports clients in assessing their current status and whether or not they are setting realistic goals. It is during this stage that clients will look not only at external barriers and circumstances, but also at their own inner incongruities, and habits that might have served to jeopardize their progress in reaching their goals.

Creating an empowerment vision: If you can't create a vision of the life you want, how can you possibly bring it into reality? A vision is where one is headed, and how one gets there is the mission statement, its goals and its objectives. A projected vision is a picture of a client's true self in the future and includes all the important elements of their life. Recovery coaches help clients build an empowerment framework through visioning.

Exploring options and resources: At this stage, a coach will guide and support clients in exploring all the resources, options and courses of action at a client's disposal that can help them accomplish their goals. Clients are encouraged to leave critical judgments aside: *"I can't afford that,"* Or *"I'm not* *that capable."* The goal here is to get clients to generate as many ideas as possible.

Developing an action plan: This is the point where discussions and plans are converted into decisions and then hopefully, action. Coaches help and support clients in envisioning and putting together a strategy that can take them from where they currently are in their sobriety and where they want to be in the near or long term future. The coaching process provides the direction needed in order for change to take place in clients' lives.

Monitoring for success: The coach serves as a guide and accountability partner. His or her role is to point out dangerous or self-defeating areas clients wouldn't normally see for themselves or are too timid to confront. Coaches also serve as monitors of the progress being made from time to time and guides clients through those kinds of impasses.

(William R. Miller and Stephen Rollnick 2013. White W. and Boyle M, 2005.)

THE INITIAL INTERVIEW

Recovery coaching begins with the first interview. The more you know about your clients the better and the sooner you can be of help. The process of recovery coaching can take many steps, and begins before the client comes in for the first appointment. It is important to realize through a client's initial application that he or she may have recently been incarcerated, has been through a contentious divorce, or court-ordered to a coaching program by the judicial system. Understandably, they may be feeling anxious, upset or angry when they come to their appointment. Let clients know at the outset that they don't have to rush into coaching until they understand what coaching is or isn't. They may need to talk a bit, and get a sense of who you are and for you to learn a bit about them.

Be sure to explain how recovery coaching works and answer any questions about what the client can expect from you and the coaching process in general. Some of the discussion will revolve around fees, appointment times or basic confidentiality procedures as required by law. Some discussions will revolve around basic informed consent procedures as required by your professional ethical code. This is also a time for the coach to begin establishing the partner relationship as the coach being someone who is open, honest, and transparent about the coaching process. Additional tips include:

1. Establish rapport with client.   Define limits of confidentiality.
2. Assess general demographic factors: male, female, etc.
3. Assess levels or types of drug use prior to treatment.
4. Utilize the 4E process: Engage; Encourage; Empower; Evaluate. *(see next page)*

The 4E Process

The 4E process serves to establish a positive relationship with a coach's clients. The process is comprised of **E**ngaging clients to comfortably express their concerns and feelings about their situation. Once coaches identify the problem, they **E**ncourage clients to reach out and take a few risks and begin exploring options and setting realistic goals. In the exploration process, coaches are also **E**mpowering clients to step out a bit more and consider the next steps and action plans. The fourth E is **E**valuation. Coaches must evaluate not only a client's progress, but their own in terms of staying on course as both move forward. In all of this, coaches are instilling a sense of hope in the future and boosting a client's morale and self-confidence. We cannot force clients to change. We can only show them the way and invite them to change. Their future is up to them. And, in essence, isn't that the nature of recovery coaching? *(Prochaska and DiClemente(1995). Changing for Good.)*

Now that you've gotten the client into your office and introductions have been made, what's next? You may want to begin by asking, *"What is causing you concern (problem) and how is it affecting you?"* Ask the client to talk about his or her concern like one would tell a story: a beginning (how it all started); middle (what have you been doing to cope or correct it); and an end (where do you wish to be). This is also a good time to begin asking clients about their goals and aspirations.

Establishing rapport is critical in the first client encounter. Show care and concern about the client as a *person*. Be sincere and genuine. It is always a good idea to only take brief notes as too much writing disrupts the flow of conversation. Be patient with clients who may fear sharing personal information at their first meeting. Always listen intently. Turn your *what-am-I-going-to-say-next* switch off.

Outlining the Recovery Coaching Benefits

It is important to articulate to a client from the very beginning what recovery coaching is and isn't and the role you will play in coaching the client.

Coach: *"We are not a counseling or therapeutic program. We don't treat anyone. We are an aftercare recovery coaching program. We take over where residential or outpatient treatment left off. You may now be ready for some type of aftercare that can help you prepare for a life of sobriety through stepping back and looking at some of your behaviors and thinking habits that may no longer be working for you and replacing them with some that do:*

- ✓ *"My role is to take you where you are today and where you want to be tomorrow. We don't dwell too much in your past."*

- ✓ *"Our relationship will be based on honesty and accountability."*

- ✓ *"We will explore internal and external barriers that get in the way of a full recovery and devise options that may personally work for you."*

- ✓ *"I will outline and help you explore community support systems that may be able to remove any barriers you may be facing."*

- ✓ *"I will help you find solutions or we will create them together."*

- ✓ *"I will help you identify any thinking errors and help you modify them."*

- ✓ *"I will provide you support and accountability for your own wellness."*

- ✓ *"Together, we will explore self-discipline strategies that can help you maintain your sobriety."*

- ✓ *"Together we will construct a personal relapse prevention plan."*

Client Screening Questions

Questions asked during orientation and the first interviews are designed to a achieve two things: 1) help clients articulate their needs and goals; and 2) to screen for client and coach safety. Some clients may express experiences related to violence and a coach has to determine if the client is worth taking on or having to address mandatory reporting issues (discussed in Laws and

Ethics module.) The coach does not want to ask these questions in an officious manner, but instead questions can be dispersed throughout the orientation interview:

- *"How can I (we) be of help to you?"*
- *"What do you expect to get from our sessions?"*
- *"What are some of your addictive habits?"*
- *"If a miracle was to happen and you were free of any addictions what would that look like?" (client: "I don't know")*
- *"If you did know, what would your answer be?"*
- *"How has that been working for you?"*
- *"Have your addictive choices helped you cope in healthy ways?"*
- *"What have been the legal consequences of your addictive habits?"*
- *"Explain how your drug use has interfered with family, job, school."*
- *"How do you see your drug use as a (or NOT) a problem?"*
- *"Briefly outline your goals and aspirations."*
- *"What would have to happen for you to be able to achieve them?"*
- *"Who could help you achieve…?"*
- *If "X" wasn't an issue would you be better able to…?"*
- *"Why did you choose now to consider making a change?"*

Do's and Don'ts of the Initial Interview

1. Approach the session from a point of respect for where the client is at.
2. Apply the MMFI Rule: *Make Me Feel Important.*
3. Establish a rapport or general understanding of the client's point of view.
4. Don't argue with, minimize, or challenge clients. You may be pushing them into something they may not be ready for. Just interact with a neutral phrase: *"Interesting, tell me more."*

5. Begin the session by setting and clarifying the client's agenda: "How can I be of help?" Or, "Where would you like to begin?" Or, "What do you expect to gain from our coaching relationship?"

6. Don't over-praise clients or give false assurances. They may be unable to accept praise, even if sincerely offered, and feel therapy will be a *feel good*, *touchy-feely* process rather than a *working* process. Offer hope, but don't make false promises. Instead, use phrases such as: *"There are no promises, but let's see what we can do together to come up with some options..."*

7. Interpret, but don't diagnose. Limit yourself to a simple, nonthreatening interpretation of what the problem might be based on from what you have heard or observed thus far. Simple interpretations (or reflection) serve to illicit clarification and test the client's insight while gauging a client's ability to accept some personal responsibility for the issue or problem: *"What I hear you saying then is____. Am I correct?"* Then follow up with an "*Interesting. Tell me more.*"

8. Ask leading or open-ended questions. This keeps clients focused on the issue and helps clients explore a problem further that just responding with a *yes* or *no* answer: "How can you describe for me what you mean by feeling discouraged?"

9. Don't take copious notes. New coaches are often violators of this axiom. Taking notes can be distracting for both coach and client. Try and wait until the coaching session has ended and the client has left before putting everything down on paper.

10. Be aware of client resistance. Resistance is a way clients protect themselves from painful experiences. For the most part resistance can be a healthy and natural process, but a prudent coach needs to begin working on a client's resistance gradually.

These are perhaps the most basic tips of the initial interview. There are other skills used in the coaching process that will be provided in subsequent modules. For now, just do your best to avoid:

- Exclamations of surprise, over-concern, or doubt.
- Flattery and excessive praise.
- Moral judgments or criticisms.
- Expressions that may be interpreted as punishment, impatience, false promises, bragging, or threatening.
- Expressions that may be interpreted as blaming, rejecting or shaming.
- Quick interpretations, advice and psycho-babble in the first meeting.
- Timid or uneasy in explaining the coaching contract to the client. Time must be taken to ensure that the client understands the entire coaching process.

Always begin with a warm, strong handshake as you introduce yourself. Once you have gotten the basics out of the way (fees and meeting times) it is time to begin the orientation discussion. This is where your qualifications are outlined and why the client picked the right person for the job. Please refer to the Appendix for a sample coaching contract that can be used by coaches to kick start their first orientation or initial coaching session. You are welcome to modify it in a manner that suits your organization or private party use.

On the following page is a *Lifestyle Questionnaire* that can help shape the coaching relationship. The questionnaire is designed to trigger a discussion that reveals bit by bit what the person being coached is about and how they think and function in the world. It is a relational process, where the coach tries to garner as much information about the client so as to better shape the relationship and get improved frame of reference about what the client feels is the crux of his or her problem and a bit of what brought the client to coaching.

NOTES

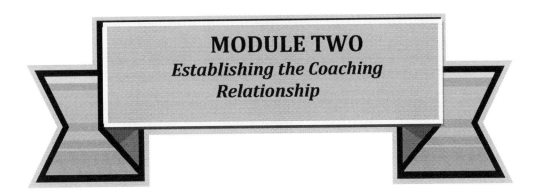

MODULE TWO
Establishing the Coaching
Relationship

This module will enable coaches to:

➢ Gain knowledge of the differences between the therapeutic, 12-step, and coaching recovery paradigms.

➢ Acquire an understanding of how the different forms of universal spirituality can serve as an adjunct to recovery.

➢ Recognize that recovery coaching is not a one-size-fits-all model and takes a spatial, non-linear approach.

A VARIETY OF CARE FOR A VARIETY OF NEEDS

No one particular aftercare support group is going to be perfect. But as Earnie Larsen, mentor and author of <u>Now That You're Sober</u> once said, *"Addicts and alcoholics who try to recover on their own are in bad company."* While safely cocooned in treatment, recovering clients become used to a predictable structure, and a regular schedule of activities and duties. But as we all know, treatment environments seldom mimic real life. Once the clients graduate, and are released to their home environment (where presumably addiction began) they are faced with having to develop major lifestyle changes and begin building new relationships that will support their sobriety. Once these issues are addressed, the process of recovery can begin, be it through Twelve Step, additional therapy, counseling or some other form of aftercare maintenance. I'm willing to say that no one program will ever cure substance abuse 100%, but as previously stated, recovering persons who utilize aftercare help in any form have a greater propensity for keeping their disorder in remission.

The question of what type of aftercare is the best fit for a client is four-fold:

1) Which model is capable of maintaining a solid foundation for a lasting recovery?

2) Which model builds upon what was taught in treatment so that once out, clients can springboard onto other life goals that can make their investment in treatment and recovery worthwhile?

3) If a program's goal is to support and increase abstinence, does it have the data that supports increased abstinence?

4) Is the program practical, affordable, and does it make sense in today's thinking?

Let's make a few comparisons

12-Step programs	Counseling/Therapy	Recovery Coaching
. Personally invested in the steps and sponsor-sponsee relationship. . Non-therapeutic. . Guidance in incorporating 12-steps in daily living. . Not a substitute for counseling or coaching. . Usually works with people active in recovery. . Quasi-spiritual paradigm.	. Professional investment. . Therapeutic, trauma focused. . Focuses on relief of emotional and psychological pain. . Not a substitute for sponsorship. . Addresses past issues and how past issues affect the present.	. Professional investment. .Non-therapeutic; client focused. . Focuses on increasing clients' motivation to reach identified goals. . Not a substitute for therapy, counseling, or sponsorship. . Addresses present issues and focuses on future goals. . Focuses on removing barriers to recovery. . Emphasizes holistic recovery.

Counseling and therapy

Counseling and therapy operate from a pathological/medical/clinical paradigm and are about looking back and finding the root causes of emotional pain and suffering. The goal is to explore the underlying cause of a client's pain and *fixing* the problem, usually through psychotherapeutic, treatment-based solutions. The problem with this paradigm is that addiction cannot be fixed and it doesn't fully go away with therapy or counseling. Much like diabetes, addiction can only be contained and monitored for remission. Because aftercare for any type of compulsive disorder or addiction requires on-going (often long-term) commitment, the therapeutic paradigm can be very expensive, time consuming and seldom offers options and rarely includes a plan for sober skills building and self-accountability in extending one's sobriety. The therapeutic paradigm is also less interactive with the therapist almost always in a top-down position serving as the expert.

Anecdotal reports have pointed to therapists telling clients that only 2 out of 10 persons will make it and then blaming the client when a therapeutic approach became unproductive, failed or the client-therapist relationship was not present. These clients are then referred to A.A. or N.A. without any further treatment. *(Baldwin Research Institute, 1998; Diana Chapman-Walsh, Harvard School of Public Health, 1995. Henry R. Miller, University of New Mexico; 1995. Linda C. Sobell & John A Cunninghan; 1993)*

However, we can't throw the baby out with the bathwater. It has also been noted that therapeutic models, when done through an extensive outpatient treatment program (with high personal accountability), can still play an important role in the care of recovering clients. For persons who may still be experiencing lingering psychological pain and feel a need to resolve past traumas, a therapeutic paradigm may still serve a worthwhile purpose.

Twelve Step Programs

As a refresher, the Twelve Step paradigm was originally developed by Alcoholics Anonymous (A.A.) in 1935 and has often been described as a linear, spiritual-based, life-long process that uses a set of twelve sequential guiding principles or steps to help clients work through their sobriety. It uses the concept of a sponsor-sponsee relationship to help recovering persons work through their sobriety. Both the sponsor and sponsee are members of an exclusive club who have paid the highest dues possible to join: alcoholism and addiction. In a sense, both are there to support each other's sobriety with the one with the most time in the program serving as sponsor.

What some critics see as limiting about 12-step programs and disempowering to some clients is that these programs carry a public stigma of being too dogmatic and people find it difficult to admit weaknesses to a group of strangers while having to embrace "Higher Power" thinking.

Another issue has been that twelve-step programs are often the default referral mechanism initiated by the court system, and because it is the first intervention option recommended in lieu of incarceration or loss of driver's license, 12-step immediately becomes associated with punishment to many people. Most people adjust to it, but many don't. Those that don't adjust have complained that while all the time they had spent sitting in a room disclosing their moral mistakes while hugging a box of tissues, their minds were still doing time.

There is also the "rock bottom" myth mentioned by critics of 12-step. If one fails the program or relapses, it was NOT because the program failed, but because the client had not yet hit rock bottom or did not adhere to the "steps". Remember that we are dealing with a disease that can be fatal. Why must we wait until one hits rock bottom to intervene, and what if that rock bottom is death?

Still, it is important to add here that for many alcoholics and addicts, 12-step programs provide a clear path away from the ravages of their disease. I must also repeat that *any* type of aftercare is a good thing. Whatever works for you, works. *(Partial sources: Drs. Marc Kern, David Foster Wallace, Alan Marlatt, and Charlotte S. Kasl: Many Roads One Journey: Moving Beyond the 12 Steps.)*

Recovery Coaching

Recovering clients need more focused attention and direction. As previously stated, we are dealing with a new using population that may not respond well to linear, sequentially designed cookie cutter programs. Today's recovering population needs to be assured that they are neither crazy nor morally deficient just because they are chemically dependent. That said, for persons with addictive behaviors who feel they don't need the circular nature attributed to therapy, and are not quite ready for 12-Step ideologies, recovery coaching may work for them.

To build on our earlier (ICF) definition of recovery coaching, one could surmise that recovery coaching is about the present, with an eye toward the future, and more about growth...not rescuing individuals.

There is no right or absolute way to recover from an addiction. Recovery coaching is unlike any traditional aftercare program in that it is not a packaged *one-size-fits-all* and believes there are several paths to sobriety. Unlike therapeutic models, recovery coaches view clients as whole individuals, not as a collection of broken and fragmented parts in need of fixing. Recovery coaches are not therapists, counselors, or spiritual gurus. They do not treat anyone, or advocate for any specific psychological principle or sequentially linear doctrine.

Recovery coaching takes a more nonlinear, client focused approach that has as its center the belief that with guidance and support, the client is the expert on himself and has the innate ability to reach self-identified goals that can lead to a sober lifestyle. It has with it an interactive, Socratic style of conversing with clients, and is more about helping clients identify any external and internal barriers in their present condition that stand in the way of reaching their dreams and goals. It goes through a process of challenging those barriers or beliefs and exploring options that will get clients to those identified goals and acting on those options.

Coaching is said to be more educative than therapeutic; solution-focused rather than problem-focused and for some clients it can be short-term, usually six to twelve weeks, although it is recommended that clients participate during the first twelve crucial months of recovery. It is a logical, low-cost link to community-based aftercare, and is designed to serve as a continuation in the process of change that was begun in treatment and can now continue in the clients' familiar home environment.

RECOVERY COACHING AND SPIRITUALITY

Individuals recovering from addictive behaviors frequently cite spirituality as a helpful influence. However, little is known about whether or not spirituality could be incorporated into formal treatment in a manner that is sensitive to individual differences. Recovery coaching isn't so much about secular solutions to problems nor is it against spirituality and Higher Power thinking. Recovery coaching is more against linearity; sequential codes of belief. Recovery coaching <u>does</u> recognize the role that spirituality can play in recovery and often encourages clients to at least maintain an open mind regarding the augmentation of several spiritual paths as support in aftercare.

Evidence has been accumulating over the past couple of years showing that the relationship between spirituality and recovery can no longer be ignored. Recent anecdotal and focus group studies with recovering alcoholics and addicts are increasingly pointing to spirituality as playing a critical role in their recovery journey. Only until recently has the role of spirituality in facilitating successful addiction treatment outcomes been identified as an area of potential importance to addiction research and clinical practice. *(National Institute of Health NIH, 2010)*

For example, recovering clients who have nurtured any form of spiritual experience have been found to be more open to suggestions as to how to incorporate mind, body and spirit *(prayer, meditation, contemplative reading, volunteering and other life-affirming spiritual activities)* into their new sober life.

Some clients have reported that this form of spirituality has given them a sense of strength they may have never experienced before.

More studies have begun to surface showing that recovering persons who have integrated practical scientific aftercare with a holistic form of spirituality in their sober journey seem to have extended periods of sobriety, make better informed choices, and are less prone to relapse. Despite the scarcity of formal research in this area, spiritual concepts have been shown to be a significant and independent predictor of recovery and/or improvement of treatment outcomes in recovering individuals. I don't have the data to prove it, but one can surmise that an integrated system of aftercare, the severity of any consequences as a result of a relapse are more short-lived and less severe because of that integration. *(Royal Ottawa Hospital Aftercare Study, 2003. National Institute of Health, 2010)*

It comes to no surprise, then, that recovering persons who integrate their recovery with some form of spiritual centeredness are considered by some as unique. They have overcome obstacles that most of us would never overcome. They are fortunate to have gotten their lives back, and most have been willing to pay that debt forward. They have adopted some pretty good standards for living that should go beyond the recovery community and be made a part of our whole culture, addicted or not (*Letting go; practicing forgiveness; one day at a time mentality; and the precepts of the serenity prayer, to name a few.*).

It is important to clarify at this point that *Starting Point* holds a broad range of personal viewpoints on spirituality and religion, including secularism. We cannot draw any hard and fast conclusions about spirituality from our research, other than it suggests a framework for future studies.

The driving force behind writing this unit of the handbook was more out of a curiosity about how recovering people view the integration of treatment with spirituality.

In doing so, we can only highlight that any form of spirituality when kept in balance with modern-day technologies, has promise and works to provide us with enough spiritual contentment, fulfillment, a sense of wholeness, wellness, purpose and happiness needed to enjoy life to the fullest. And isn't that the goal of recovery?

THINGS NEEDING CHANGE IN RECOVERY

Albert Ellis, the father of Cognitive Restructuring was once credited with saying, *"Only nuns change their habits overnight."* This is applies to recovery coaching in that very little happens overnight. Upon entering recovery from drug and alcohol addiction, recovering persons are hit with a range of immediate changes that need to be made, especially in the five life domains that may be affected by people, places, and things associated with a client's learned habits. This is where clients will need a coach's skill and support.

Negative patterns have been established over months or years of neglect in recovering clients. By conducting chalk-talk exercises periodically, clients tend to become better prepared at considering changing their old lifestyles and their erroneous thinking patterns and beliefs.

As your clients go about developing their personalized plans, remember to stress honesty. Honesty is the best way to reveal any negative thoughts and behavior patterns so that they can proceed to make healthy and realistic changes in their lives.

Making Lifestyle Changes

About People
1. Who in your life is it difficult to separate from?
2. Who in your life has been associated with your addiction?
3. How could you begin communicating to these people that you are working to stay sober and that they need to respect that?
4. Who in your life would you like to get closer to?

Places

1. List the places you need to avoid.
2. Why do you need to stay away from these places?
3. Name some healthy places you could visit.

Things

1. Name five things that remind you of using that you need to get rid of immediately. (music, paraphernalia, etc.)
2. List three things you will have to change in order to reduce the triggers you will face.
3. Why is it important to change the things related to your addictive habits?

Thinking and Beliefs

1. List five things that create negative attitudes and thoughts relating to your recovery journey.
2. How does your thinking trigger you into using again?
3. Describe how you are handling anger triggers in your recovery.
4. List three things you can begin doing to avoid anger triggers.
5. Why is it important to change the way you think?

What if I Relapse?

This is a common question among recovering people. Relapsing should not be the end of your journey. Recovery coaching sees relapse as a temporary setback, a stage of change, and a learning experience. Learning to live all over again can be a tall order when one considers keeping all five life domains balanced, especially during the first year of recovery.

I have found that the longer a client participates in a solid aftercare program, the shorter relapse episodes become. Subsequent relapses, if any, also become less severe in terms of consequences because of what was learned in the recovery process. Much of what is taught in recovery coaching in relapse avoidance involves acquiring clarity, gaining new life skills and having a new and balanced vision for your life.

Maintaining Our Life-Balance (exercise)

It is a good practice to review with clients (and with yourselves) at periodic coaching sessions what they are doing to maintain at healthy levels our recovery capital in each life domain. The tips below will help you and your clients monitor one's life-balance.

Physical: Don't burn yourself out. Avoid exhaustion by getting some down time. Follow a consistent food plan and get plenty of rest and exercise. Exercise helps you sleep better.

What am I doing to maintain a balance? _____

Mental: Don't entertain self-defeating mind trips. Get rid of all the unnecessary baggage you have stored away. Avoid rationalizing or minimizing your recovery journey. You will never get a third chance at a second chance. Learn ways to stimulate yourself intellectually. Read up on recovery. Take a college course. Keep mentally active.

What am I doing to maintain a balance? _____

Emotional: When troubled and unsure as to how your recovery is going, ask for help. Don't bottle up your feelings by letting them build up inside you. Emotional baggage can be defined as painful memories, mistrust and hurt carried around from past abuse, control, or emotional rejection. Join a support group and use that forum to express your feelings and emotions. Most of all, avoid people (relatives included) who do not support your recovery journey. Be patient with those you hurt and brought sadness and sorrow to during your drinking and drugging days. Earning back trust is a long and challenging process.

What am I doing to maintain a balance? _____

Social: Begin building sober relationships. Don't let yourself get bored. Boredom opens the door to relapse events. Also get out and meet some people through volunteering, get involved with things that bring you joy and contentment. Be a giver and not a taker. Learn a hobby; join a bicycle club...just do! The internet is chock full of sober contacts.

*What am I doing to maintain a balance?*_____

Spiritual: Pray, meditate, do both. This is a good time to begin building recovery capital in the spiritual element for the challenging times ahead. Do something good each day for someone less fortunate. Tutor students in low-income communities. Work at a food bank. Spirituality can encompass both faith and values. One does not have to be a religious person to be spiritual. Some of the most spiritual and giving individuals do not actively practice an organized form of religion. What they do is set a spiritual example through their deeds. You do not have to be better or perfect or be anything you're not. Your beauty is in you, just as you are each moment. When in doubt, go within and believe in yourself and tap into that part of you that is Spirit...God. Celebrate your successes and your growth.

*What am I doing to maintain a balance?*_____

Everyone, especially persons in recovery, wants to be happy, but as we have demonstrated in the lessons above, sometimes we tend to cling heavily to unnecessary baggage that gets in the way of our recovery and that can throw us off balance. Remember that what is left of your drug-free life requires only one piece of carry-on luggage. The rest is unnecessary. There is a Zen quote that goes: *The best time to plant a tree was 20 years ago. The second best time is now.* "QUOTE"

EIGHT THINGS TO GIVE UP IN RECOVERY

It's time to kick that excess baggage to the curb. As coaches, we can begin to brainstorm with clients on how to look at their erroneous thinking habits (baggage) and behaviors by helping them step back and begin taking a long hard look at what some people may interpret as character flaws, but which I like to refer to as *interesting characteristics*. This is nothing more than unnecessary baggage which up until now has been blocking their ability to pursue a life of happiness. They include:

The need to always be right. Those who refuse to admit their mistakes will struggle to grow in recovery and may soon relapse.

The need to control things and others. One of the most important things learned in any aftercare program is to let go of people and things you cannot control. By letting go of things out of your control will greatly improve one's recovery life.

Blaming others for your misgivings. One must take responsibility for our own lives. Blaming others does not lead to any progress in recovery. Blaming persons, events, and external things is giving away your power.

Fighting Change. Change happens and we have little control over it. It is an unstoppable force of nature and fighting it almost always leads to suffering.

Obsessing about the past. What's done is done. Yesterday is history, tomorrow is a mystery. Live for today and make each day memorable.

Complaining about one's recovery journey and life. That accomplishes nothing and only drains one's energy and motivation. It is what it is so just make the best of it.

Listening to self-limiting beliefs. Stop selling yourself short. People who settle for bare minimum, only get the bare minimum. You don't like what you've been getting? Then change what you've been doing.

Refusing to let go. Letting go of baggage is not an easy task for anyone. Abandoning one's comfort zone is doubly painful. We fear what lies ahead because it is unknown, unpredictable, and has little or no reference to evaluate your next move. The past is familiar and reliable. But if any change one makes is familiar and comfortable, then it isn't really change is it? So don't worry about the past and clinging to old baggage. Just forge ahead and your future will find you just by letting go of your past.

(*Sources and inspiration: The Buddha; Bill Keane; Shakespeare; Olympia Dukais, Pope Francis.*)

 **CHALK TALK**

Which baggage are you willing to give up? (exercise)

Begin exploring some real or imagined baggage of your own (or your clients) and how you may have coped or combated them:

 Listening to your self-limiting beliefs:

 The need to always be right:

 Complaining about our recovery journey:

 Obsessing about your past:

 Fighting change:

 Refusing to let go:

CHALK TALK

LIFE STYLE QUESTIONAIRE

You are what you practice. Please take the time to review and practice or role play each exercise at the end of each module. Starting Point does not leave training to chance. Coaches who do not reinforce their training through real life application and practice are, in reality, making poor use of their investment.

About Yourself

1. What have been your three most significant accomplishments?

2. What have been your three most significant disappointments?

3. What three things (people, results, resolutions, etc) do you want the most right now in your life?

4. What three things in your life are causing you discomfort or stress?

5. Which one of the above would you like us to start coaching on first?

6. How would you describe your current state of well-being?

7. Looking forward six months, describe three goals you have achieved as a result of your coaching experience? How do they look?

8. Describe any goals you have yet to fulfill.

9. Of the above goals, which one is most important to you?

10. What is it about you that people like the most?

About Life

1. What are the three biggest concerns/fears about life?

   _____

   _____

2. What motivates you to want to improve your life?

   _____

3. What are the three most important things you have learned or accepted about yourself?

   _____

4. What are the five things you currently have to tolerate the most and how are you dealing with them?

   _____

5. What is it about you that makes your life work as well as it does?

   _____

6. Who are the key people in your life and what do they provide for you?

   _____

7. Is your life of your own choosing or is it based on circumstances?

   _____

8. What is it about your day that you like the most? The least?

   _____

9. What else, if anything, do you feel is important to accomplish in order for your life to be fulfilled and complete?

   _____

   _____

About Client History

1. What have been your three most fulfilling accomplishments thus far?

   _____

2. What has been the greatest obstacle you have had to overcome?

   _____

3. How have you failed in the past and how did that affect the way you think today?

   _____

4. How have your attitudes about people and life changed over the past five years?

   _____

   _____

5. What has made you the most successful or powerful?
    _____
    _____

6. Are you mostly past-, present-, or future-oriented?
    _____
    _____

7. What should I know about your professional background/history?
    _____
    _____

8. What should I know about your personal/family background?
    _____
    _____

9. How well are you doing in life's five areas: physical, mental, emotional, social & spiritual?
    _____
    _____

10. How willing are you able to grow and explore greater possibilities?
    _____
    _____

(Sources: The coaching Starter Kit; The Coaching Tools Company; Aaron Beck; Fowler International Coaching Academy; Starting Point Wellness and Recovery Center; National Recovery Resource Center.)

Karma Clean-up

➢ **The first to apologize is the bravest.**

➢ **The first to forgive and forget is the strongest.**

➢ **The first to let go is the happiest.**

"Let go of your baggage. This trip only requires one carry-on."
(Dr. Lou)

MODULE THREE
Recovery Coach Competencies

This module will enable coaches to:

➢ Explore levels of coaching competencies.

➢ Gain knowledge of the concept of *change*.

➢ Examine how a coach structures the coaching relationship.

➢ Outline coaching benefits to clients.

➢ Explore the concept of *presence* and *commitment*.

RECOVERY COACH COMPETENCIES

It has been said that a great recovery coach is one who can play tennis on the same side of the net as his client as tennis balls are coming at him at 110 miles per hour; meaning that recovery coaches have to be right there alongside their clients when the going gets tough. Recovery coaching is about empowering clients to take action in their lives and will require specific qualities, characteristics and competencies from coaches that can determine what leads to successful working alliances.

Professional traits can vary, from coach to coach. There are some common qualities inherent in all coaches that play a critical role in affecting the bond that is created between coach and client that allows self-awareness to occur, chemistry between coach and client being the first. Second, the old *'been there, done that'* assumption that a coach who has had alcohol and addiction issues in the past is of greater benefit to the coaching process is not totally accurate. It may serve one well in a mentor-mentee relationship, but not always as a professional recovery coach. Granted, a large percentage of recovering persons have things in common that helped them overcome the challenging aspects of recovery (*individualism, empathy, intelligence or at least streetwise, and creativity*), but without any core, foundational competencies these innate characteristics will only serve to limit their ability as professional recovery coaches.

General Characteristics

In their studies on the characteristics of persons working in the mental health professions, Benjamin Chapman, David Linden and other mental health professionals characterized successful counselors, trainers, and coaches as sharing six key common traits:

1. **Empathetic listener** – the ability to reflect back the emotions clients are expressing so that clients feel they are being heard and understood.

2. **Extraversion** – associated with warmth, assertiveness, and higher levels of positive emotion.

3. **Openness to experience** – individuals who exhibit a wider range of experiences are more curious about the world. Those who value a wider range of client experiences and positions are more likely to develop trusting relationships with their clients.

4. **Observant** – being able to identify thinking patterns in clients by observing and listening to inflections in voice and then there is body language.

5. **Emotionally-balanced** – open and participative in give-and-take exchanges.

6. **Conscientious** – the ability to demonstrate competency, order, and responsibility to the task at hand inspires confidence in clients.

(Sources: Benjamin Chapman, David Linden, Terrence Gorski, David Loveland, Bonnie Dubrow)

There could be other characteristics of a more general nature, to be sure, but in recovery coaching there is a basic body of core competencies one must possess in order to become effective coaches. In their research, Chapman and Linden point to recovery coaches, as possessing three major core competencies:

✓ personal
✓ professional
✓ community

Below are key concepts that are of vital importance to the change process:

Personal Competencies
- Having an open mind or personal belief that there exist several paths to recovery.
- Is a good listener and possesses a fair to good sense of humor.
- A genuine demeanor that easily connects with people.
- The ability to establish empathy with clients.
- Comfort and an ability to work with diverse populations, cultural backgrounds and community settings.
- A functioning B.S. detector.
- A natural curiosity and interest in others.
- Comfort in working independently across disciplines.
- Ability to focus on and reinforce positive strengths and behaviors in clients.
- A high level of energy and commitment to the coaching process.

Professional Competencies

There are certain cognitive similarities among stigmatized and marginalized people, recovering clients being among that group. They are steeped in self-delusion, irrational thinking, self-doubt, shame, and counterproductive attitudes (learned helplessness). These similarities require coaches to have at the very least a familiarity of a variety of scientific approaches that address those issues. The following core professional competencies support a greater understanding of the professional skills required of recovery coaches working with recovering/stigmatized/marginalized clients:

- A familiarity with chemical use, addiction, and mental health issues.
- Working familiarities of the relapse process, its challenges and prevention and intervention techniques that address relapse.
- A working familiarity with focused-questioning used in the pursuit of thoughts and ideas that lead clients to a point or a goal.
- Knowledge and understanding of non-conventional, psycho-social paradigms such as: Cognitive Restructuring, Reality Therapy, and Cognitive Behavioral Theory (CBT) to name a few.

89

- A working knowledge of the Stages of Change Theory: How clients can be made to move from a position of ambivalence to one of change.
- Solutions-focused Questioning: asking coping and solution-focused questions that empower clients to action.
- Anger avoidance while in recovery: Few professionals know that addiction and anger go hand in hand and must be addressed simultaneously if a client is to fully recover. Learning to avoid personal and environmental anger triggers and dealing effectively with the frustrations brought on by the mere nature of sobriety is key to a successful recovery.

Community-Based Competencies

Because recovery coaching takes a more non-linear, integrated approach to recovery, coaches will have to provide assistance through an array of programs and services in the community they serve, and connect clients to other (sometimes competing) resources to meet specific needs. It is not uncommon for a client who feels he or she can benefit from attending Alcoholic Anonymous or some other aftercare program and recovery coaching with you simultaneously. Recovery is about the client's needs, and not that of the coaches. Some key community-based competencies include:

- Knowledge of faith, cultural and gender-specific community resources that can support a client's recovery.
- Access to resources: child care, food shelves, transportation, bus tokens, safe houses for battered women, clothing, shelter and affordable housing.
- Knowledge of and access to community systems that support recovery: affordable housing, education, employment, mental health services and legal advocacy, interventionists, counseling services and food shelves.
- Resources for training, education and employment.

 **A Word of Caution**

Don't set yourself up for failure by attempting to incorporate all twenty or so competencies simultaneously or try to incorporate them into your professional life all at once. That would be too heavy of a load to carry. Merely circle one or two each week and practice them. Arrange these competencies in your head as you work with clients. Memorize, but don't compartmentalize.

(Sources: David Loveland, Ph.D. Syllabus for Recovery Coaching and Personal Recovery Plan Development, (1996); Terence T. Gorski, Staying Sober (1986); CENAPS; International Coach Federation and Recovery Coaching International. Louis D. Gonzales, Ph.D. Starting Point, Inc. Benjamin Chapman, Personality, Characteristics of therapists. (May, 2009) Journal of Social and Clinical Psychology.)

BEING PRESENT AND COMMITTED

In recovery coaching we find clients grasping at past or present, and real or imagined disappointments as a justification for NOT moving forward. They claim they could win their battles if it weren't for all the physical and mental barriers that are conspiring against them. They find themselves thrashing about for solutions, but they can't connect with anything solid and as a result place themselves at greater risk of relapsing. Recovery coaches play an important role in helping clients work through their initial stages of recovery as they collaboratively work at finding solutions to removing those barriers that prevent them from reaching their goals. In recovery coaching it is called *Cognitive Restructuring*; restructuring or rewiring the way one thinks about recovery and life. Finding someone who is dedicated to providing practical, aftercare guidance can often be a great challenge for clients.

From the onset, coaches should begin establishing co-creative relationships. That is, by establishing trust and presence with their clients. Presence is a form of caring, dedication, listening, focusing, and serving as an accountability partner with the client. Coaches are like loyal, metaphorical seeing eye dogs as they guide clients through a process of shifting perceptions from limited, *either-or* choices to *these-those* array *of* choices, opening a world of options and opportunities.

How to Demonstrate Presence and Commitment

The primary role of the coach is to create a safe, supportive environment that fosters mutual trust and respect. Below are a few examples:

- ✓ Listens more; talks less.
- ✓ Demonstrate respect for clients' perceptions/opinions/learning styles.
- ✓ Has genuine concern for clients' welfare and future.
- ✓ Provides ongoing support and champions the learning of new behaviors, taking risks and celebrating those risks when they pay off.
- ✓ Is flexible during the coaching process (dances in the moment).
- ✓ Goes with his or her gut feeling (trusts own intuition).
- ✓ Uses humor effectively and appropriately.
- ✓ Uses analogies and metaphors to illustrate a point (paints verbal pictures).
- ✓ Confidently explores new directions with clients.
- ✓ Is clear, articulate, and direct when sharing or providing feedback.
- ✓ Is the accountability partner and clearly monitors clients' commitments and keeps the session(s) moving in a forward direction.

(Adapted from: International Coach Federation (ICF)

Phrases That Promote Presence and Commitment

Giving encouragement:
- ✓ *"I believe that you have the inner strength to meet this goal."*
- ✓ *"You're doing great. Keep at it."*
- ✓ *This will get better soon."*
- ✓ *"Don't even think about giving up."*
- ✓ *"I understand. It seems that whenever you try something new, something like this happens."*
- ✓ *"Don't listen to the naysayers. Two clowns don't make a circus."*
- ✓ *"Stick to it...especially now."*

Creating anticipation:
- ✓ *"What are the possibilities?"*
- ✓ *"What if it worked?"*
- ✓ *"What does your intuition tell you?"*
- ✓ *"What is realistically possible?"*

Showing empathy:
- ✓ *"How are you feeling about it right now?"*
- ✓ *"Let's keep working on it together. We'll get through this."*
- ✓ *"When was the last time you had a similar challenge?"*
- ✓ *"How did you handle it?"*

Clarification techniques:
- ✓ *"Where did you learn that?"*
- ✓ *"Says who?"*
- ✓ *"How do you know that for sure?"*
- ✓ *"What's most important to you right now?"*
- ✓ *"If there was a solution, what would that be?"*

Refocusing the problem:
- ✓ *"Let's focus on what's working."*
- ✓ *"How might you be able to let go of....?"*
- ✓ *"How long has this been going on?"*
- ✓ *"What do you want most to happen?"*
- ✓ *"You seem to be stuck on this goal. Let's find a more doable one."*

Readiness:
- ✓ *"Are you ready to begin?"*
- ✓ *"What's the first step you can take?"*
- ✓ *"What is the first thing you should stop doing?"*
- ✓ *"What can you begin doing on a daily basis?"*
- ✓ *Who do you trust that you can begin asking for help?"*

Exploring resources:
- ✓ *"What resources do you have that could help you decide?"*
- ✓ *"What kind of vision is going through your head right now?"*
- ✓ *"Who could you reach out to that could help you...?"*

(Adapted from Tony Stoltzfus, Jerome Daley; *PurposeCoaching.net*; Phillip Sandahl.; Co-Active Coaching, 3rd edition; *John Whitmore: Coaching for Performance, the GROW Model*)

Focusing on Client Needs

Once clients are encouraged to express in words what is going on inside them, they can then be helped to consider options, solutions, and next steps to finding solutions to their internal and external obstacles. An effective coach listens for clues focusing on what the client is saying and what the client is NOT saying:

- Focus on getting more information: *"What are your challenges and how are they affecting you?"* Or, *"Is there one key obstacle here? Interesting, tell me more."*
- Focus on motivation: *"What brought you here?"* Or, *"What is the least (or most) that you would like to achieve by being here?"* Or, *"You've found it hard to make this change. What do you gain by not changing?"*
- Focus on thoughts: *"When you experience that problem, what do you tend to think?"*
- Focus on feelings: *"When you are thinking that way, what do you tend to feel?"*
- Focus on urges: *"When you feel that way, what do you get the urge to do?"* Then follow up with, *"How is that working for you?"*
- Focus on goals: *"What have you done in the past that has helped?"*
- *"What do you consider a successful outcome of this session?"*

Begin to assess the time for change. Do not move ahead when clients are not ready. Remember that it their agenda, not yours and they decide if and when it is time to move on.

Remember: focused listening is always about whom, what, where, and when, but <u>never about why.</u>

(Sources: Miller & Rollnick. 1996 & 2013 3rd edition; Starting Point Inc.; Buzzle. Com; Tony Stoltzfus: Leadership Coaching.)

Orientation Discussion Sample #1

Thank you for taking the first step in your desire to begin rebuilding a newer and better life for yourself. That must have taken a lot of courage. I just want to let you know up front that you have all the power needed within you to make the changes you need to make to reach your goal(s), and my job will be to help you find that power. Tell me briefly, what is it that you would like to work on during our coaching sessions together? (discussion held)

First, I need to let you know that I am not a therapist. I don't do treatment, I am a recovery coach. By that I mean that I am about growth and not rescue. I don't go into your past. My concern is about your present situation and your future. I don't provide you with answers, but through the work we will do together, I hope to help you find your own answers.

As your coach I will maintain a professional, collaborative relationship that will focus on your strengths and abilities to conquer or cope with whatever is preventing you from meeting your goals or your dreams. Our relationship will be based on trust, support, experience, mutual accountability and on helping you regain or achieve a life you once dearly loved, but was lost through your addictive or compulsive behaviors. This is what I am prepared to do with you:

- ➤ *I will help you grow from where you are today to where you want to be.*
- ➤ *Part of what you will be getting from me as your coach is a fresh, experienced pair of eyes.*
- ➤ *Together we will explore options and develop an action plan for meeting those goals you have set for yourself.*
- ➤ *Together, we will explore solutions to the external or internal barriers that are getting in the way of meeting your goals.*
- ➤ *I will be your accountability partner and call you on any discrepancies you may be expressing in our sessions. I will fact check, help you clarify issues, and support you in making better decisions.*
- ➤ *I will help you sustain your strength and stability at higher levels so that you can reduce your reliance on substances or other compulsive habits.*
- ➤ *You will have access to a sensitive listening partner through email, Skype, or telephone.*
- ➤ *I will be your conduit to your definition of success.*
- ➤ *Does that make sense? Are you ready to go to work?*

Orientation Discussion Sample #2

"Let's take a hard look at how you got here. I don't have all the information yet to make any assertions, but from what I've heard thus far, many of your problems may be related to addiction. Is that correct? Did you begin drinking and drugging to deal with your problems? Your drinking and drugging seem to have evolved into an addiction and that placed you in treatment. Correct? And now you are worried that your addictive behaviors will return and you fear a risk of relapse. Is that somewhat correct? [Conduct a discussion]

I am very happy that you chose to seek some form of aftercare. Here's what we will do together: I'd like you to identify problems or challenges and together we will see how they relate to your addictive thinking and behaviors. We're going to discuss how you have been trying to manage them on your own. Together we're going to look at ways you can begin challenging some addictive thinking habits and develop more rational ways of thinking. And finally, we are going to work together at devising a personalized plan of action to support you, or at least help you cope with the challenges that may arise in recovery. I will ask that you self-monitor by telephone, contacting me by email or telephone to fact check a thought, urge or idea. I will become your accountability partner and together seek out ways to remove any barriers that are getting in the way of that happy life you deserve. Does that make sense? Are you ready to work with me?"

"I didn't like what I was getting, so I changed what I was doing."
(Alcoholics Anonymous)

 EFFECTIVE ORIENTATION QUESTIONS (exercise)

You will want to review the points given during the orientation session and begin to find out what the client wants to work on the most. Listed below is a handy list of topic questions that can be asked during the first weeks of coaching:

Problem Identification

Directness in a positive manner is essential to the recovery coaching process:

- ✓ "What is your most pressing challenge or concern and how is it affecting you or others?"
- ✓ "What has led up to this?"
- ✓ "What part did you play in all this?"
- ✓ "What are you (or others) doing to cause or complicate the problem?"
- ✓ "Why are you interested in solving the problem now instead of the first time it happened? (follow up with discussion)
- ✓ "Describe how this problem may happen in the future if it is not solved."

List three ***problem identification*** questions of your own:

1._____

2. _____

3._____

Clarification Questioning

- ✓ About the problem: "You said you had difficulty with…Tell me more about it."
- ✓ Thoughts: "When you experience that problem, what do you tend to think?"
- ✓ Feelings: "When you think that way, how does it make you feel?"
- ✓ Urges: "When you feel that way, what do you have the urge to do?"
- ✓ Actions: "When you feel that urge, what do you actually do?"
- ✓ Relationships: "In doing so, how does it affect your relationships?"
- ✓ Whether it's working: "How do these actions get you what you want?"
- ✓ Change what you're doing: "Share with me another way to cope with the problem/situation."
- ✓ "How much is…affecting your personal happiness?"
- ✓ "How much longer are you going to put up with…?"
- ✓ "What is this problem/challenge…costing you?"
- ✓ "How does that behavior affect your (job, family, marriage)?"
- ✓ "How much does that take away from your (significant other, family, etc)?"
- ✓ "What would you like to change about your situation?"
- ✓ "What effect(s) does drinking or drugging have on your relationship with…?"

List three **_clarification_** questions of your own:

1._____

2._____

3. _____

Empowering Questions

- ✓ "If you want to get along better with…, what approach might be more effective?"
- ✓ "How have you handled this sort of thing in the past? Would that work today?
- ✓ "How do you think you and I might work through this problem together?"

List three _empowering questions_ of your own:

1._____

2._____

3._____

Consequence & Alternative Questioning

✓ "What is the worse (or best) that could happen?"

✓ "What's the most likely thing that will probably happen?"

✓ "Who will be affected the most from any decision you make?"

List three consequence/alternative questions of your own:

1._____

2._____

3._____

Options Questioning

✓ "If you had any choice what would you do?"

✓ "What are the possibilities that you could consider?"

✓ "What have you done in the past to help solve this problem?"

✓ "What has been helpful?" "What has not?" "What seems to make things worse?"

✓ "Name five ideas that could help you solve this problem."

✓ "Of your five ideas, name two that you are certain would help solve your problem."

✓ "Which idea would you choose?"

✓ "Why is it important for you think the way you do?"

List three **_options question_** of your own:
1._____
2._____
3._____

Setting Expectations

No expectations = no follow through. During these first sessions it is always a good thing to help your client become used to your coaching style and expectations. Some of the more successful coaches come across as honest, supportive, and frank (yes, frank). They pull no punches, but always have the clients' interest at heart. You begin by:

1. Reviewing the ground rules, agreements, and terms of the relationship.
2. Reviewing and have client sign the ninety day agreement.
3. Collecting the first month's payment.
4. Designing in advance three goals or self-improvement projects to work on the first 30 days.
5. Determine where on the path of recovery the person is at.
6. Identify the current barriers to the clients' success.
7. Give the client one or two skill assignments to practice each week.
8. Tell the client what you will do together in the current session. When the session has ended, tell the client what you will do together in the next session.
9. Schedule the next/subsequent sessions.
10. Send a "*I look forward to working with you*" e-card.

List some of your expectations regarding your own coaching sessions:

1. _____
   _____
2. _____
   _____
3. _____
   _____

CHALK TALK

Structuring the Relationship Role Play Exercise

Role play with your coaching buddy an orientation scenario you may have been involved with in the past by recreating examples you have previously listed. Then switch sides and repeat the exercise.

1. Question that sets the agenda:

   _____

   _____

2. Getting clarification of the problem:

   _____

   _____

3. Giving encouragement:

   _____

   _____

4. Showing empathy:

   _____

   _____

5. Causes questions:

   _____

   _____

6. Refocusing the problem:

   _____

   _____

7. Readiness:

   _____

   _____

NOTES

This module will enable coaches to:

- ➤ Describe why a bond between coach and client is critical to the change process.

- ➤ Understand and illustrate recovery coaching's value and acceptance process.

- ➤ Understand aspects of multicultural coaching.

- ➤ Identify and discuss techniques for working across cultural groups.

MULTICULTURAL BONDS

The most impactful activities coaches engage in are engaging, encouraging and empowering clients. In coaching across cultures and lifestyles, the interaction between coach and client clearly becomes an added component critical to the coaching process. Not understanding or ignoring this concept all together will hinder a coach's ability to connect with his clients regardless of ethnicity or lifestyle.

The active interactions (the 4E's) that occur in coaching sessions represent two thirds of the program; the remaining third is the chemistry that exists between the coach and client *(Wampold & Bhati, 2004, R.J. Chapman, 2003, et al)*. Printed materials and provocative videos without solid and trusting interactions do little to change behavior.

The persona of the coach can be of greater significance to the coaching process and can be the central ingredient for creating a bond and effecting change in clients. Just as dynamic teachers facilitate greater student achievement, dynamic coaches achieve better results with their clients. Genuine curiosity, focused listening, passion, and an excitement about the opportunity to work with others can create a spark that makes people, regardless of cultural background, want to work with a coach.

MULTICULTURAL COACHING

Unless you're Native American, broadly speaking, all of us are multi-cultural beings. Here's a quick gut check. How do you feel about people of other races or cultures, religious beliefs, GBLT, the homeless, dreadlocks, tattoos or piercings, inter-racial or same-sex marriage, persons with HIV, or the handicapped and those from the East coast, Midwest or the West coast? They all have their own cultural distinctions. Multicultural means just that: many cultures.

Were the feelings conjured up in your head as you read the above a bit biased? Cross-cultural bias is the phenomenon of interpreting and judging others by standards inherent to one's own culture. The phenomenon is sometimes considered a problem central to social and human sciences.

The term multicultural was once restricted to one of the major races or cultures. Today multicultural has taken on a broader meaning. Whether we admit it or not, the assumptions we make about the clients we serve often spill over into our professional interactions with others in subtle, and sometimes not so subtle, ways. The growing increase in racial and cultural diversity in treatment and aftercare has made cross-cultural competence a necessary standard in current health and human services training programs.

What is Multicultural Competence?

Multicultural competence is a set of congruent behaviors, attitudes, and policies that come together among professionals or in a system which enables effective work in multicultural settings. It is a way of thinking and willingness by professionals to adapt to the needs of clients, and to meet those needs in objective and non-judgmental ways.

Numerous biases exist concerning cultural norms of color, physical handicaps, sexual or religious preferences, language, and other cultural taboos. The behavioral sciences especially have had a history of protecting the status quo against change, and have been slow to respond to the evidence of culture bias in their treatment protocol. At least this has been the perception of many practicing minority professionals and others in the cultural competence movement (NAMI, Multicultural Action Center, et al).

Bias and ethnocentricity in recovery coaching is no different than in the other behavioral sciences. Biases and ethnocentricity can often contribute to our inability to meet the needs of diverse clients as they work at developing effective recovery and life plans for themselves. Xenophobic attitudes in these areas almost always influence the treatment outcomes of clients of diverse backgrounds.

Modern-day, psychodynamic approaches may not be as congruent with these populations as some cognitive approaches used in coaching. It is rare to get less acculturated clients in a group process primarily because they harbor fear of exposure to what might be perceived by others as weaknesses or shortcomings due to ingrained beliefs surrounding gender roles, a clear patriarchal family hierarchy or religious beliefs. We are beginning to learn however, that when psychodynamic are repackaged i.e., more client-centered and respectful of the clients' background and beliefs, and in a manner that clients can understand, chances will increase that less acculturated clients may become open to participating in coaching.

I have learned that storytelling and analogies, for example, are highly valued in many non-western cultures. When using a story to make a point, always ask your clients, *"What did this story (or analogy) mean to you?"* or, *"What experiences have you had that helped you learn this lesson?"*

Coaching Persons of Diverse Backgrounds

How does one become culturally aware in substance abuse services and subsequent aftercare programs? As a result of rapidly changing demographics in this country, and as professionals in the new business of aftercare and recovery coaching, we need to explore effective and appropriate ways of serving clients of diverse backgrounds.

For example, how does one communicate effectively with clients of other cultures or lifestyles about sensitive issues such as sexuality, drug use, and violence in family relationships? How do coaches incorporate a client's life experience in order to ascertain the underlying causes of their behavior, which at first may be guarded or not readily apparent? How do we empower them to move from a position of deficit to one of self-empowerment? These are all questions coaches are beginning to ask themselves. Interviewing skills and rapport building are paramount when working with diverse populations as the wrong comments or tone could make clients retreat into their self-protective behaviors and possibly dismantle the coaching process.

Culturally aware coaches always begin by respecting their clients' cultural self-determination and identification and devise ways of fusing their behavioral techniques with their clients' cultural values. It is important to understand that family and community in most cultures are seen as important institutions, and for some cultures, God-given gifts that need protecting. Be aware of the family hierarchy when coaching across cultures.

Culturally aware coaches also refrain from imposing direction and judgment or using a voice of authority with clients, as doing so creates barriers that may impair the coaching relationship. Taking a course or workshop on cultural diversity can be an ideal first step in understanding your clients better. It is also important for our mental well-being to not become discouraged as we maneuver through any new cultural territory. Remember that cultural competence is a life-long developmental process and we are always learning.

Establishing Multicultural Relationships

Coaching across cultures can be challenging, but not impossible. For example, in our effort to learn and understand as much as possible about our clients we tend to muddy the coaching process by asking irrelevant and sometimes inappropriate questions. For example: *"Where are you from? What tribe do you belong to? I have several gay friends and..."*

We must take the time to pause and listen carefully to what our clients are saying (or not saying). Less acculturated clients like to check us out first, and that's understandable. They almost always ask themselves questions about the coach as a person and less about the coach's professional strengths. That is because they are not so much interested in our credentials, as they are in trying to locate our world view and how it applies to how we can help them. The meta-message with persons of different cultures and lifestyles might be: *"As we engage in this activity you call coaching, tell me which perspectives, life experiences, and values you are coming from that tell me that you have a sufficient understanding of my culture to help me, the person."*

Building Client Rapport
  ➤ Engage clients in a warm, respectful manner. Don't interrogate.
  ➤ Be aware of family hierarchy.
  ➤ Don't stereotype.
  ➤ Avoid the one-size-fits-all theory when coaching.
  ➤ Refrain from imposing direction or using an authoritative voice.
  ➤ Respect clients' rights and cultural self-determination.

- ➤ Reflect empathy, not sympathy. (Been there-done that doesn't always work.)
- ➤ Avoid using humor until you have been given non-verbal permission.
- ➤ Seek to understand clients' goals from their cultural perspective.
- ➤ Be aware of levels of multiculturalism in family constellation. (1st generation may speak English in public, but their home language with family.)
- ➤ Become aware of the impact xenophobia, and poverty might have had on the family.

Examples of working across cultures:

It is important to take the time to gather all the information you can about the clients you will be coaching:

- ✓ What is the client's dominant language?
- ✓ What is the cultural communication style?
- ✓ What is the family hierarchy and roles (patriarchal or matriarchal)?
- ✓ What are the gender roles?
- ✓ What is their spiritual base?
- ✓ Is alcohol or drugs used in their religious or social rituals?
- ✓ What are (or have been) their traditional health care practices?

Take the First Steps in Acceptance

Be genuine and always engage clients in a warm and respectful manner. Try to always communicate respect and optimism. The Washington University Center for Multicultural Education suggests that persons working in multicultural setting take the first steps in acceptance by doing the following:

- ✓ Increase your knowledge base about the clients being served.
- ✓ Avoid addressing clients in too informal a manner. Less acculturated clients expect a more formal, but not too rigid relationship with people they do not know well. In time, and if the process works for them, you will be given non-verbal cues as to whether or not to take on a less formal posture.
- ✓ Dress business casual. People in the helping professions are still viewed by most cultures as authority figures and business or formal wear may represent a threat or an air of superiority/disapproval of the client's current condition.

- Reflect empathy, but do not disclose your past compulsive behaviors (drinking or drug issues). The old *been there, done that* approach does little to create self-awareness in any form.
- Avoid using humor until you have been given non-verbal permission to do so. Humor, when used to take the client's mind off an emotional subject or threatening problem, may communicate that the statements or revelations clients have made are unimportant.
- Do not fall into the trap of offering solutions. Authority figures are expected to direct and tell people what to do. Because you will be viewed as the authority figure (at first), less acculturated clients will expect you to tell them what to do in their recovery efforts. Keep reminding clients that the solutions are within them and that your role is not to give direction, but to guide them in the direction of their goals.
- In coaching sessions where families are involved, it is always a good idea to develop an awareness of who is the final authority. In some cases, the mother may be interacting with the coach, but you will find that the father may be the final authority. But do not assume that the male figure is always the one in charge. One incorrect assumption may destroy the whole coaching process. Use your best judgment.
- Seek an understanding of the client's goal from his or her own perspective first. Listen for clues as to possible influences of cultural and spiritual beliefs.
- Determine the impact that external barriers such as xenophobia, poverty and acculturation have had on the family. Many clients have survived insurmountable barriers just to get make a better life for their families :
    - The struggle of just getting to the U.S., some crossing two borders.
    - Adjusting and forging new lives in a new and alien environment.
    - Having to cope with the stressors of xenophobic attitudes, rejection, exploitation and racism that up to now may have made substance abuse almost a necessity, but be careful here.
- Determine the level of multiculturalism within the family constellation. Discuss the appropriate hierarchy in your clients' culture/ethnicity, family, or community (only to determine the role of the male/female clients in the coaching process). Parents may hold on to rigid cultural values, but their children may straddle both the American and home culture.

✓ When possible and appropriate, try to learn a bit of the cultural identity of the clients, but do so carefully because it may not matter depending on the enculturation or sophistication of the client.

Building Multicultural Understanding

There are numerous cultural nuances in recovery coaching, and they all have individual meanings and importance to the clients you will be serving. Always pause, think, and ask yourself: "How is this information going to help (or impact) the coaching process?" For example, substance abuse might be in conflict with the clients' personal identity and values; it might conflict with the values of the community's spiritual or religious beliefs or the family structure. It is important to know in advance how substance use plays in the roles of family, religious groups, celebrations and the community's attitudes such as drinking at weddings, baptismal and *Quincienera* (sweet fifteen celebrations) in Latino communities and how those values will affect your clients' aftercare process, for example.

✓ Become proactive in the community you serve and combine forces with other local agencies and organizations.
✓ Become aware of lifestyle, cultural and ethnic networks within the treatment process: community reinforcement support (extended family networks, faith-based principles, motivational interviewing, holism, fellowship-based programs, the Medicine Wheel, 12-step), and the roles and stressors of being from a patriarchal or matriarchal society.

Empathy and cultural understanding are learnable skills for understanding a client's meaning in a coaching relationship. As in any coaching setting, it is the building of a trusting relationship between coach and client that is key.

Of course, no professional can ever know all that is relevant about every cultural group, but the core to multicultural competence lies in respect for differences, an understanding of diverse points of view, and a willingness to consider and incorporate cultural differences in your work.

Now that we are rapidly becoming a pluralistic society, cultural competence should be a standing ethical commitment in all areas of health and human services by mere virtue of how different cultural groups are when defining health, illness, and health care, for themselves, especially in the context of mental health and substance abuse.

(Sources: Thompson, M., Ellis, R., & Wildavsky, A. 1990; Sue, D.W.,& Sue,D. 2003; NAMI. National Alliance on Mental Illness; 2004. Evidence-practices and Multicultural Mental Health.2001. Louis D. Gonzales, Ph.D. 2008.

Below is a Lakota tale that serves as a metaphor for the whole notion of acceptance. Take a few minutes to discuss its meaning with your coaching buddy.

A Lakota grandfather was teaching his teen-age grandson about life. As they sat at the bank of river waiting to catch the fish that would bless their dinner table, the grandson asked, *"Grandfather, why is it that sometimes I feel like there are two wolves inside of me snarling at each other; one telling me good things and the other urging me to do wrong. At times I don't know which one to listen to. Why is that?"*

The grandfather commented: *" There is a fight between those same wolves going on inside of every person,"* he said to the boy. *"It is a terrible fight. One represents evil, anger, envy, greed, arrogance, bias, resentment, and false pride. The other represents joy, peace, love, hope, inclusion, humility, kindness, and generosity."*

The grandson thought about it for a moment and then asked, *"Which wolf will win, grandfather?"*

The grandfather paused and replied, *"The one you feed."*

(Anonymous Lakota Tale)

MODULE FIVE
The Coach as Change Agent

This module will enable coaches to:

➢ Explore and describe the Stages of Change.

➢ Understand and define *Intentional Interviewing* principles.

➢ Gain knowledge of and describe how Intentional Interviewing helps clients move from a position of ambivalence to one of *change*.

➢ Explore and practice key change-talk techniques for creating change.

STAGES OF CHANGE IN RECOVERY

Change comes slowly to people struggling in recovery. It is a process that takes time and commitment. It is built on multiple capacities, strengths, resources, coping abilities, inherent values and is highly personalized for each individual. Because recovery is non-linear (doesn't follow simple sequential steps) and involves setbacks, part of recovery coaching is to foster resilience for all individuals involved in making critical life changes. But not everyone may be ready for change, and if they are, it can happen at different stages.

Over the years, there have been several stages of change models being offered by researchers *(e.g. Horn, 1976; Rosen and Shipley, 1983; et al.)* We have chosen the works of Prochaska and DiClimente as the main source for two reasons: 1) their model has generated more research than the others, and 2) their model better outlines our need for an understanding of the stages persons with substance use disorders go through when they're faced with making life changes.

Seven Stages of Change

Recovery coaches are change agents; skilled at surveying their clients, accessing which clients are at various levels of change and why learning the Stages of Change Model is an important tool for getting clients to self-search, question their motives, resolve their ambivalence, and begin moving forward in their recovery.

Seven Stages of Change model, expanded from research conducted by Drs. James Prochaska and Carol DiClimente wherein they outline five (5) stages individuals go through in addressing their readiness for change. <u>Recovery Coach Academy has added two important stages critical to substance use recovery: 6) Relapse; and 7) Transcendence.</u> These two have been added because the body of research in addiction aftercare and our own professional experience support the fact that recovery is based on continual growth with occasional relapses or setbacks, and those setbacks can be used by clients as stages of learning and change. Transcendence here is being used as a term for "crossing-over" as a better way of looking at recovery and NOT an *end* to or termination of any addictive disorder which we have already learned cannot be ended, but only kept in remission. Let's look at our integrated version:

Pre-contemplation – The denial stage (*"I don't have a problem."*). Clients may be ambivalent about participating in the program. They may be attending against their will or may be in denial about having a compulsive or substance use disorder in the first place. It is a good idea that at each session or during a break, you ask for progress feedback, *"How are you doing with all this?"* or *"Are you finding this helpful?"*

Contemplation – The client is thinking about participating, but is at the teeter-totter stage: *"Should I or shouldn't I? Maybe I am using too much, but I'm not sure… but even if I am, I am not sure I'm ready to do anything about it."* Wait the client out. Hopefully he or she will come around and you will be working as a team. Remember that change is a fluid process.

Preparation – The client likes what is happening and is getting ready to participate: *"Hell, I've got to do something anyway. It can't hurt. I can't go home empty-handed."* Relax. Only a small change is needed herefor the client to begin to accept more change.

Action – The client has made a conscious decision to commit: *"Let's do this thing!"* When change begins to happen, always ask empowering questions such as, *"What made you decide…?"* or *"Awesome! How did you do it?"* and *"What did you do differently?"*

Maintenance – The client likes the results of the program and is practicing maintaining new behaviors. It is about clients getting into a solid, sober daily routine. The changed behavior is now becoming the *normative* behavior.

We should pause here and highlight two additional stages affecting recovery and addictive disorders:

Relapse – This is the *"uh, oh!"* stage (followed by a groan). Clients may have gotten sloppy with their program or began to feel over-confident in maintaining their new behavior that they took a chance and relapsed. It may be that the skills leading up to the new behaviors were done sporadically (practice creates habit), and clients now see themselves as moral failures.

Assure your clients that a relapse may occur in anyone's sober journey, but that they aren't moral failures by any means. A relapse should be a learning and growth opportunity. Although the change process Prochaska and DiClemente describe appears linear, in practice it is not. It is not uncommon for a person to temporarily regress to a lower stage (relapse) given the nature of the person's level of commitment to change or life circumstances. What is important is that we take the time to analyze what led up to the relapse, how was it handled, and learn from it. Relapse is a natural, learning stage in the change process.

Transcendence– This is considered by some as the liberation or final or termination stage. Because recovery is a life-long process, I prefer to call it the *transcendence* stage; a going beyond, rising above… a realization of a new life, but not being fully liberated. I say this because an addiction is never fully terminated. Like diabetes, it can be held in remission, but it never fully ends. Those in long-term recovery refer to it as the *"I can live without it"* stage. This is where self-efficacy has increased to the level where the change has taken on a lifestyle of its own and addictive thoughts are no longer an integral part of a person's life, and returning to old addictive habits now seems atypical, abhorrent and as young clients put it, *weird.* It is important to keep reminding your clients to remain cautiously optimistic at every stage.
(Sources: Prochaska, J., Norcross, J., & DiClemente, C. 2013. Gonzales, 2014. Gerald J. Connors, 2011. M. Velasquez. 2013)

EMPOWERING CLIENTS TO CHANGE

It is important to note that up until now, your clients have experienced great failure at self-change and may become demoralized by another change notion that may place them at risk of yet, another failure. Take it slow. Remind clients that the reason they may have failed in the past could have been due to their trying recovery on their own without the proper support, or that their goals were set too high or were unrealistic to begin with.

Try to communicate a sense of hope to your clients; that with your guidance they can begin to rediscover their inner strengths and, with a little work, change what was once impossible. An effective coach helps clients arrive at this stage by working as a co-investigator alongside the client and by asking motivational questions that elicit change-talk. The goal is to have clients come to a realization and articulate their aspirations and goals by exploring an array of options available to them.

Giving Support

As you have read, readiness to accept change is a result of the quality of interaction between coach and client. Below are examples of showing signs of support, and motivational questions that can empower and elicit change-talk in clients.

Empowerment and support:

✓ *You're doing great! Keep going.*
✓ *See, you've got what it takes.*
✓ *Stick with it.*
✓ *It is going to get better as you go.*

✓ Don't listen to the naysayers (two clowns don't make a circus).

Showing empathy

Miller and Rollnick define empathy as: The extent to which a coach communicates accurate understanding of the client's perspectives and experience:

✓ *It must be tough.*
✓ *It seems like it's _____.*
✓ *That happens to a lot of people.*
✓ *I can only imagine how that must feel.*
✓ *That must make you feel _____.*
✓ *Not to worry; we'll get through this. It's okay, really.*

Clarifying what works

✓ "What is already going well and doesn't need to change?"
✓ "Can you name some assets or good qualities about yourself that...?"
✓ "Name two things thus far that have given you the strength to..."
✓ "What needs doing to make that happen?"
✓ "How exactly will you do that?"
✓ "What do you see as a next step?"

Being more intentional

✓ *"Who owns this problem?" or "Who is involved in this problem?"*
✓ *"What are others doing to cause or complicate this problem?"*
✓ *"What have you done to complicate this problem?"*
✓ *"Who are the players that can help solve this problem?"*
✓ *"How is this problem affecting you or other people?"*
✓ *"When did this problem first start?"*
✓ *"Describe how this all came to be."*
✓ *"How does this problem relate to the greater problem...?"*
✓ *"How does this problem make it harder to practice and stay focused on your program?"*
✓ *"Do you think that the need for external validation has anything to do with...?"*
✓ *"How does your problem create in you an urge to think about old addictive behaviors?"*

(Sources: Prochaska, J., Norcross, J., & DiClemente, C. 1995; William Miller and Stephen Rollnick. 2013). Fredrike Bannink, 2004. Alan Ivey, 2010; Tony Stoltzfus, 2001).

Getting clients to open up and consider any kind of change can take some time and a lot of hard work, but it can be made easier through engaging clients in conversation and drawing out their ideas that can cause them to consider changing the way they look at their recovery process and life. It is about a coach putting the pen down, removing the notepad off his lap and actively listening to a client, eye ball to eye ball, and asking the right questions. This is not a revolutionary principle. It just takes a little work on the part of the coach.

INTENTIONAL INQUIRY

*I*ntentional Inquiry is one of the best basic coaching tools used to promote wellness in clients. Intentional Inquiry (I.I.) takes inspiration from the Motivational Interviewing (M.I.) paradigm developed by Drs. William Miller and Steven Rollnick to promote insight and awareness in clients, and is about making observations and bringing to a client's attention *(through Socratic or focused questioning)* discrepancies and incongruities that are apparent to the coach, but unaware to the client. Both M.I. and I.I. an attempt to challenge incongruities between clients' goals and their behaviors and help clients arrive at logical conclusions. Both use a similar theoretical lens in promoting interactive communication, insight and awareness to clients. Let's just say that both I.I. and M.I. questioning styles have complementary principles and can often used interchangeably.

I.I. however, is a bit more direct *(but not confrontational)* with the intent of guiding, promoting insight, and challenging clients to consider questioning their own incongruities and faulty thinking while exploring more neutral or positive options. The main goal of I.I. is the resolution of ambivalence and eliciting "change-talk".

Cognitive Incongruities found in clients

There are six common types of cognitive incongruities described in the literature that are commonly observed in clients:

1. Discrepancies between a client's verbal and nonverbal message.
2. The incongruity when the client makes a statement that contradicts what was already stated.
3. The incongruity between a client's personal beliefs and actual experiences. For example when a client expresses a belief, but their actual life experiences contradict their belief. (*"I'm quitting drugs and enrolling in college…"*but he keeps using.)
4. The incongruity between personal value system and their outward behaviors.
5. The incongruity between what the client says and how he chooses to behave.
6. The incongruity between their earlier life experiences and their future plans. (despite having bad experiences in the past, the client continues to make the same choices that once got them negative experiences).

(Cormier S. (2012) *Counseling Strategies and Interventions.* Ivey A.E. (2012) *Basic Influencing Skills; Essentials of Intentional Intervewing. Allan S. Bakes 2012)* Helpful Strategies for Teaching Effective Confrontation Skills.)

Using I.I. to draw out change-talk

Change talk can best be described as being interactive and collaborative. The coach is an empathetic co-investigator along with the client encouraging the client to become an active participant in the change process. It begins by asking the client purposeful, open-ended questions that get to the root of a client's problem. *("How does your problem interfere with what you would like to do?")* While there are many variations in technique, basically the spirit of Intentional Interviewing revolves around four basic principles:

1. Motivation to change is never imposed by the coach, but drawn out from the client.

2. The I.I. process is designed to promote self-acceptance and one's ability to produce insight... results.
3. The coaching style is generally calm but purposeful.
4. The coach challenges and supports clients in their efforts to examine and resolve their own ambivalence.

Intentional Interviewing Highlights:
- ✓ Involves collaboration, interaction and exploration, but not authority or recommendations.
- ✓ Can be direct and in the spirit of interest and concern for the client.
- ✓ Focuses on intentionality and flexibility.
- ✓ Points out discrepancies between clients' goals and their behaviors through questioning and the collaborative exploration of solutions.
- ✓ Clients identify the behaviors they want to change.
- ✓ Coaches help clients identify the benefits of change.
- ✓ Realistic and attainable goals are set.

  Coach encourages self-accountability for goals set.

(adapted from, and suggested reading: William Miller and Stephen Rollnick. (2013) *Helping People Change; 3rd Edition.* Allen Ivey., Mary Bradford Ivey, et al. *Essentials of Intentional Interviewing* and *The use of Confronting as a Microskill.*)

Intentional Interviewing Techniques

The key which underpins Intentional Interviewing, according to current literature *(Ivey, Bradford, Miller)*, is that the clients are the experts on themselves and of their situations and, through intentional guidance, are more likely to make changes if they are guided and empowered to work things out for themselves. It may sound a bit Gestalt-ish, but the secondary goal is to reduce resistance to insight in clients by getting them to accept the *here and now* of what is happening in their lives. A third and final goal is to elicit change-talk in clients by helping them connect seemingly unconnected dots and coming to a "burning bush" (or Aha!) moment. What follows is a working example of Intentional Interviewing techniques:

Setting the Agenda by determining the target behavior:

- "What would you like to talk about today?"
- "Where are you right now with...?"
- Let's get down to business. Last week we discussed..."

Clarify the agenda around a target behavior about which there is ambivalence, through asking clarifying questions:

- *"So you feel_____."*
- *"It sounds like you___."*
- *"I'm getting a vibe that you're still not ready to…. am I correct?"*
- *"I get from listening to you that you have the innate capability to…"*

Ask about the positives: This is often an engaging surprise and helps mold the relationship.

- *"What are some of the good things about _____?"*
- *"People repeat certain behaviors doing because there is something that has benefited them in some way. How has _____ benefited you?"*

Always summarize the positives:

- *"Well, it sounds like something is working for you."*
- *"Talk about the pluses of your confronting the____."*

Ask about the negative aspects of the target behavior:

- *"Can you talk about the downside of _____?"*
- *"What are some aspects of your options you are not so happy about?"*
- *"What are some of the things in your changes or adaptations you would not miss?"*

Explore life goals and values:

These goals will be the pivotal point against which cost and benefits are weighed.

- *"What sorts of things are important to you?"*
- *"What sort of person would you like to be?"*
- *"If things worked out in the best possible way for you, what would you be doing a year from now?"*

(Use affirmations to support "positive" goals and values.)

Summarize:

- *"Let me see if I can summarize what I just heard."*
- *"What is your conclusion?"*
- *"What does all this amount to?"*
- *"How would you describe your efforts thus far?"*

Ask for a decision:

Restate their dilemma or ambivalence then ask for a decision.

- "You were saying that you were trying to decide whether to continue or cut down. What have you decided? How is that going to work for you?"
- "After this discussion, tell me what you are clearer about what you would like to do?"
- "So, have you made a decision?"

Goal setting – Use S.M.A.R.T. goals (Specific, Meaningful, Assessable, Realistic, Timely)

- *"What will be your next steps?"*
- *"How realistic are your options?"*
- *"What will you do in the next one or two days?"*
- *"Who will be helping and supporting you?"*
- *"On a scale of 1 to 10 what are the chances that you will do your next step?" (Anything under 6 and their goal may need to be more achievable.)*

➢ **If no decision is made or the decision is to continue the behavior.**

- Empathize with difficulty of ambivalence, but press on.
- Ask if there is something else which would help them make a decision?
- Ask if they have a plan to manage the consequences of not making a decision.
- If the decision is to continue the behavior, go back and explore the ambivalence.

Note: Only open-ended questions elicit change-talk and empower clients to expand on their ideas, options and thoughts.

(Adapted from: David B. Rosenberg; Alan Ivey; T. Solstzus; David Miller; Steven Rollnick; Phillip Sandahl. Mark Young, and The American Counseling Association (2012).)

CHALK TALK

Behavior Motivational Scale (exercise)

1--2--3--4--5--6--7--8--9--10

The Behavior motivational scale is used by many service providers to assess the readiness of a client to change. Practice this technique on your coaching buddy and circle/discuss where each of you are on a readiness to change.

Why is your motivation where it is? You must have had a good reason for circling that number. List those reasons below:

1. _____

2. _____

3. _____

4. _____

What steps can you take to move your scale from (add #) to (add #)?

1. _____

2. _____

3. _____

4. _____

(Adapted from: Oklahoma Assistive Technology Center)

NOTES

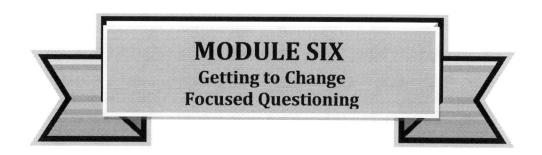

MODULE SIX
Getting to Change
Focused Questioning

This module will enable coaches to:

> Explore the concept of Socratic Questioning and how it applies to recovery coaching.

> Explore and understand the principles of:
  - *Interactive, Solutions-Focused Questioning;*
  - *Motivational Interviewing M.I. ; and*
  - *Intentional Interviewing (I.I.).*

> Learn the principles of open-ended questions that elicit change-talk.

> Gain knowledge of how to reinforce a client's forward movement toward change.

> How to apply solutions-focused questioning into the coaching role.

MAINTAINING AN EMPOWERMENT MOOD

Problem-focused talk generates problems. Solutions-focused talk generates solutions. Clients are looking to you for answers to the question," *Now that I'm sober, what's next?",* and hope that you will provide them with answers. We call this phenomenon *learned helplessness.* Many clients have spent an inordinate amount of time being blamed, shamed, and told what they ought to do and not do that feigning helplessness now comes naturally to them. Many have never been encouraged to take action on their own behalf and become their own rescuers. While cocooned in a treatment setting, clients may have learned a few basic relapse prevention or recovery skills, but are now out in the real world where clients are suddenly feeling intimidated by the standards and challenges of the sober world and the risks of relapsing have quadrupled.

Take time out of each session to remind clients that recovery coaches do not give answers, but that they collaboratively explore solutions and serve as guides in helping clients identify and achieve the goals they have set for themselves. In coaching, this is known as maintaining an *empowerment mood.*

The Nature of Empowerment

One important role of recovery coaching is the chemistry between coach and client. Solution-focused questioning (not advising) is a powerful tool for quickly defining the relationship between coach and client. Advising is never a good thing. When a coach advises, he or she becomes the expert and takes on a role of intellectual superiority over the client. But when a coach interacts in a supportive role, then he viewed not so much as an expert, but as an <u>empathetic, but knowledgeable partner and a conduit for empowerment.</u> Below are some additional tips that coaches can use to maintain a solution-focused or empowerment mood during their coaching sessions:

- **Ask goal questions.** Focus on the objectives clients want to reach in each session, or if with a group, determine what the group is wishing to accomplish over several sessions. Make sure you have a clear and specific process goal from the start or you'll lose sight of your progress: *"What do you most want to talk about in this session?"* Or, *"What do want to get out of our time together?"*

- **Let go of your agenda**. This is not about you. New coaches always seem to be looking for that Holy Grail of questions; that one question that will change a client's behavior forever. Forget about it. Just keep asking the simple questions and see where they lead. You'll often notice that the client will decide where to take your questioning if you just listen.

- **Watch your 'W's.** Always ask who, what, when and where questions, but never "why."

- **Avoid playing therapist.** Do not diagnose or label the client's state of mind. Instead ask, *"Interesting. Tell me more."*
  interrupt when necessary. You heard me right. Being too timid to interrupt or too afraid to refocus the discussion often slows the progress, but interrupt carefully, respectfully, and not too often. Part of your job is to manage the coaching process, so when you see clients bird-hopping, you need to interject with a question that brings the conversation back to focus: *Do you mind if I interrupt occasionally to keep us on track and make the best use of our time? We will have time later to visit any key concerns you may have."*

- **Never ask closed questions**. Closed questions (Yes...No) lead nowhere. Consider using open-ended questions, *"Talk to me about another approach you could take to____."*

- **Ask permission** to expand an idea or to continue to the next phase of a topic: *"How does that work?"* or *"Can you take what you just described to the next level?"* Since there is no therapeutic formula here, always follow your curiosity and you'll be surprised where it leads.

- **Never blame or shame** clients for their situation or you'll surely set yourself up for a confrontation, a shut-down, or walk-out.

- **Speak the language clients understand,** but don't speak down to them either. Never use high-end sophisticated terms or words. If you do catch yourself being too sophisticated then bring it down a notch by downplaying what those terms mean: "Don't worry about that concept for now. It just means... and I'll break it down as we go. For now it is just important that you understand that..." In some cases I find that I have to explain the term right off, and then move on.

Solution-focused questioning respectfully assumes that clients can become empowered to play an active role in their change process. Given the proper coaching, guidance, and support, they can begin to tap into their own potential and begin taking control and responsibility for their own progress. However, there are clients who are not ready, or are even fearful of sharing their hopes and dreams. It is always better to resist the temptation to fill the silence between the questions you ask, and a client's response. That brief moment of silence gives the client the respect and permission to think and reflect without you interrupting.

II. Facing barriers/obstacles:

- ✓ *"What do you think could be stopping you from...?"*
- ✓ *"What have you already done to help yourself reach your goal?"*
- ✓ *"Describe how this problem is likely to emerge in the future."*
- ✓ *"Who are the players in your life that are blocking your goals?"*
- ✓ *"What do you need to do by (or to) yourself to help remove these barriers?"*
- ✓ *"You've mentioned money three times. If you had the money you needed what would you do?"*

III. Alternative analysis questioning:
- ✓ *"What have you tried in the past to resolve this issue?"*
- ✓ *"What was helpful? What was not helpful? What seemed to make things worse?"*
- ✓ *"What if you were to consider trying...? What would be the worst that could happen?"*
- ✓ *"What have others in this group done to resolve similar situations?"*
- ✓ *"What ideas can this group think of to try helping him/her resolve this dilemma?"*

IV. Weighing the pros and cons:
- ✓ *"What are the benefits or disadvantages of sticking to your recovery plan?"*
- ✓ *"Where are these feeling you expressed taking you?"*
- ✓ *"Identify for us the three best alternatives to..."*
- ✓ *"Let's look at the pros and cons of each of the three alternatives."*
- ✓ *"What's the best that could happen if...?"*
- ✓ *"What's the worst that could happen if...?"*
- ✓ *"What is the most likely thing that will happen if...?"*

V. Questions that elicit options:
- ✓ *"What could you do about this?"*
- ✓ *"What are other courses of action you could take...?"*
- ✓ *"Give me three options for how you could solve this challenge."*
- ✓ *"Out of these three options, what else could you do? Now choose, which option looks the most doable (list them)."*
- ✓ *"What have you seen others do that might work for you?"*
- ✓ *"What other resources could you tap into that...?"*
- ✓ *"Let's get radical here. What if the obstacles were removed, what would you do then?"*
- ✓ *"Let's throw out three options that come to mind that could..."*

Make sure clients are doing all the heavy lifting. Don't let clients get stuck on just two or three options. Have them write down their first three options, and then revisit them at a later date, at which time they can explore two or three more options.

The objective here is to push the clients beyond their initial set of options and keep them locked in their creative, empowerment zone.

IV. Decision-making questions:

- ✓ *"What do you plan to do next?"*
- ✓ *"What are you willing to do to resolve this problem?"*
- ✓ *"What is the worst that can happen if you risk and try...?"*
- ✓ *"What steps have you already taken to put your solution into action?"*
- ✓ *"Are you willing to write that into your recovery plan?"*
- ✓ *"What are the signs that point toward your being ready to...?"*
- ✓ *"What kind of preparation and support will you need?"*
- ✓ *"Name five persons you can rely on for support."*
- ✓ *"Name three steps you can take with the naysayers and road blockers on your sober journey."*
- ✓ *"How will you know if your solutions worked?"*

Now is the time to test clients' creative energies by providing them with assignments that can be tested in the real world. At first, this may seem like a daunting task for clients. The good news is that they will now have the opportunity to try out their options and analyze them in the safety of subsequent coaching sessions, thus avoiding or reducing any emotional tsunamis.

INTERACTION THROUGH QUESTIONING

Interactive solutions-focused questioning is taken from the Socratic questioning principles credited to the Greek philosopher Socrates. It is less direct than Intentional inquiry in that its purpose is to explore ideas and pursue thoughts in many directions with clients. Because the technique is highly interactive, it has become effective in exploring complex ideas, getting to the core of things, and to uncover erroneous thinking habits and beliefs in clients.

It has already been discussed that recovery coaching is an interactive but inquisitive, conversational style of coaching used to move clients toward considering making a change. We've also learned that people will make the most lasting change when the decision to change is motivated internally by what they hear themselves say rather than externally from what is being said by the coach. Knowing that they have arrived at their own conclusions minimizes a client's fear of exposure and resistance. I say fear because often much of what is troubling clients is their fear of the self-disclosure (*to disclose is to disclothe*) and a fear of rejection by having to change from the *using* person they once were to the new and sober person they are now becoming.

These troubled clients have been wearing masks for so long and are now expected to remove them and expose themselves to the world. Don't get me wrong, some fear is a good thing. In fact, fear can be a great motivator in many cases, but it's a negative one. But because fear and apprehension have always been looming in the client's life, this familiar gridlock can only be exposed carefully in front of a *trusted* and *truthful* person. Trust and truth are key domains in recovery coaching.

About Trust

Trust is an important component of the M.I. process. Fear has always been a constant cloud over recovering clients' heads; fear of not being as good as others, of not living up to family expectations, fear that they may never get their former lives back; anxiety about not feeling competent enough to make that desired change, and feelings of non-validation.

Trust, then, plays a critical role in the change process. If a coach pushes too hard for change when the clients is not ready, the sound of a coach's voice alone can trigger memories of past failures which signals to the client to retreat or revert to past defense mechanisms for fear of being exposed. Coaches need to proceed slowly and be non-confrontational and it has to happen in collaboration with clients and it must be done respectfully.

About Truth

Depending on time spent with the addictive behaviors, many persons in recovery suffer greatly from delusional behaviors (and who may be very *economical* with the truth). There are some persons with substance use disorders who use lying as their default mechanism for hiding the real issues that may be getting in the way of their recovery. Lying comes normal to this group as lying is what once kept their addictions alive. These cognitive mechanisms can often be taken into the coaching arena. In recovery, it's called unaddressed delusional thinking or residual cognitive distortions. Whatever you wish to call it, truth is a key element all types of questioning (Motivational Intentional Interviewing and Direct Interviewing) and must be addressed simultaneously with recovery principles. This can often be an unpopular concept with clients in recovery for obvious reasons. Terence Gorski in his book *Staying Sober* describes relapse and recovery as having an intimate relationship and that both must be addressed openly and honestly. Relapse tendencies are almost always tied to self-delusional behaviors.

Once stabilized in treatment, it is very easy for clients to take their unaddressed delusional thinking habits into recovery, making life miserable for themselves and those loved ones who are trying to provide recovery support. It's not that they're immoral; it's just that delusional behaviors have have become their only reliable means of keeping their obsession alive, blocking out pain or getting other needs met. If those behaviors and beliefs are not dissected, challenged, and restructured, the tendency to relapse grows stronger.

I'm not great on analogies but, self-delusion can be described as the mold that accumulates in basements. Both grow best in the dark, but when they are brought out into the light, they tend to die out rather quickly.

Much of the contents of recovery coaching involves shining the flashlight on incongruities, distortions and delusions. Coaches find themselves challenging things that people feel most ashamed and embarrassed about. It is not surprising, then, that a coach will encounter a bit of resistance in the M.I. process and finds that more cognitive work may still be needed in trust-building to get clients to a point of feeling comfortable in confronting certain truths about themselves and their beliefs.

When supported by empathy and respect, pointing out cognitive discrepancies can work at breaking through those trust barriers. Pointing out discrepancies may not always be popular with clients at first, and not easy to accept, but you will find that the most straight-forward, truthful, and trusted recovery coach will ultimately make the most gains with his or her clients.

(Read Terrance Gorski's and Abraham Twerski's materials on addictive thinking and behaviors; NIDA: Relationships in Recovery).

SOLUTIONS-FOCUSED QUESTIONING PRINCIPLES

This bears repeating: Recovery coaching differs from other paradigms in that it uses more of a direct, Socratic process where one question answered is followed by another deeper question and that answer is followed by yet another deep question until the process points out cognitive distortions in what clients are expressing (or not expressing) in their dialogue. The process can be more direct than M.I. and I.I., but never confrontational. Through this direct questioning process, clients are encouraged (or nudged) to step back and take a hard look at themselves, connect-the-dots and consider an array of solutions or options to solving their current challenges. In doing so, clients are better able to step back and analyze discrepancies between their current thinking and beliefs.

Asking the *"So What?"* Questions

Pun not intended, asking *"So what?"* is a way of connecting-the-dots and getting clients to think about what they are saying and what that means to the overall problem they are trying to resolve. Solutions-focused questioning is a good method of creating buy-in and empowering people to open up in more honest ways. When a coach begins to ask solid questions or inquires about an opinion of a client, the coach is sending a message that says, *"You are the main player in this change process (not me) and you are the one that has to decide."* Solutions-focused questioning, then, invites clients to buy into the process and empowers them to do things they never thought they were capable of doing and moves them toward taking responsibility for their own change.

Solutions-focused questioning is highly interactive and all about empowering clients to consider options which may seem tough (divorce, changing living situations, life's ultimatums, etc.),but which result in change. In solutions-focused questioning, the more a coach expresses an empathetic, yet directive form of questioning, the more clients are prone to interact and move closer to selecting an option. . It increases their ability to see how capable they really are and how much change they can accomplish on their own with some encouragement.

The recovery coaching mantra could easily be: *"You have options and are accountable only to yourself. Regardless of what you have been through, you have the strength and the power within to change the outcomes."*

Interaction through "Says who" questioning

Clarifying:
✓ *Where did you learn that?*
✓ *Says who?*
✓ *So what? What would be so bad if you...?"*
✓ *Whoa! Help me understand that one.*
✓ *Are your options doable?*
✓ *What does that look like?*
✓ *Is this always the case?*
✓ *Where is the truth in this situation?*

Challenging:
✓ *How much have you contributed to...?"*
✓ *When will you reach that goal?*
✓ *Why do you think that is happening?*
✓ *Have you tried facing it head on?*
✓ *What's the worst thing that would happen?*
✓ *What's the best thing that would happen?*
✓ *So (what or who) is holding you back?*

Confronting an uncommunicative client:

- ✓ If the client changes the subject, respond with: "Can you answer my question, and then we can talk about the new subject."
- ✓ If the client only answers part of a question, then repeat the original question.
- ✓ Ask the client to repeat the answer: "Wait, run that past me again?"
- ✓ Ask if the person remembers the original question.

Moving towards action:

- ✓ *Is this a good time for action?*
- ✓ *What are your next steps?*
- ✓ *What is the first step you will take?*
- ✓ *Tell me what you're going to do.*
- ✓ *Are you ready to get to work?*
- ✓ *What will you do? When?*
- ✓ *How will you know when you have arrived at your goal?*

"The wise man is not the one with the answers, but the one with the questions."
(Bertrand Russell)

CONNECTING THE DOTS

"*W*hat evidence do you have to support your thoughts?" A very common question asked in cognitive restructuring as it applies to recovery coaching. Intentional Inquiry consists mainly of using Socratic questioning as a technique in restructuring clients' erroneous beliefs and faulty thinking habits. Recovery coaches may use a line of questioning in order to identify, and challenge the validity of clients' thoughts, beliefs and assumptions associated with their troubles.

Through the processes of M.I., I.I., and focused questioning, the coach is supporting clients in tapping into their own strengths and innate abilities as they begin to recognize the discrepancies between their current behavior and their desired goals. This questioning process quickly allows clients to connect the dots and become their own initiators and creators of the change they feel is needed.

The questioning process does not impose ideas, opinions or gives advice to clients. Instead, it communicates empathy and respect as the coach works at helping clients cut through their erroneous thinking by drawing out thoughts and ideas from clients. By connecting their own dots, clients come to that burning bush moment (an awakening) on their own, thus reducing the fear, shame and self-reproach the clients may have brought to the coaching session.

Below is a list of additional techniques that coaches can use and which have been found effective with clients in connecting the dots and creating their own change:

Ask permission. The technique of asking for permission communicates respect for clients. Also, clients are more likely to move toward change when asked, rather than being lectured or told to do so:

> *"Do you mind if we talk a bit more about that?"*
> *"Do you mind expanding on that a little more so that we can all understand it?"*
> *"Interesting. Is this a good time to put our heads together and explore some possibilities?"*

Practice change-talk. Change-talk is a method for eliciting reasons for change by giving clients a voice in their own decision to change:

> *"What would you like to see different about your current situation?"*
> *"What do you think will happen if you don't (or do) change?"*
> *"What would your life be like in three years if...?"*
> *"On a scale of 1 to 10, how are you really doing?"*
> *"What would it take to get you from (add number) to an 8, 9, or10?"*

Explore importance of, and the confidence to change. Exploring the notion of importance and confidence to change with a client or group has dual utility:

1) Clients reveal information about how they view the importance of change in their lives.
2) It gives clients a voice in their need and desire to change.
> *"How would your life be different if...?"*
> *"What would need to happen for you to...?"*
> *"What would it take for you to move from___to___?"*

Open-ended questioning. Open-ended questioning allows for a richer and deeper conversation that builds empathy with the client:

> *"Fascinating. Tell us more why you like..."*
> *"What happened since we last met?"*
> *"What makes you think it might be time to change?"*
> *"What happens when you behave that way?"*
> *"What's different about quitting this time?"*

Reflective listening. Fastest way to express empathy:

> *"It sounds like, maybe you…"*
> *"So on the one hand you say…., but on the other…"*
> *"What I hear you saying is…. Am I right?"*
> *"It seems as if…"*
> *"I get the sense that you…"*

You are not alone

> *"That can happen to a lot of people when…"*
> *"Many people report feeling as you do."*
> *"I've also read where people in recovery have experienced the same___."*
> *"How many in this room have experienced a similar situation?"*
> *"For some, it's pretty easy to fall into that trap."*

The bumbling detective approach. Also known as the Colombo technique named after the detective in the old Colombo television series:

> *"Let me see if I understand this. You are coughing your lungs out and are always out of breath, and you are saying cigarettes are not the cause of your problem. Could you explain that to me?"*
> *"So help me understand…"*
> *"Wait. Can we pause for a minute? Earlier you told us that you were…, but now you're saying… How does that work?"*
> *"Let's walk through this together once more. You say…"*

Expressing self-efficacy or competence. This gives voice to the changes (or progress) a client or group has already made:

- *"It sounds like you've really been making progress. Tell us about it."*
- *"Fantastic, and how is that working out?"*
- *"So you've cut down on your drugging. Tell us how you've been able to do that and how is that working for you?"*

Go with the flow. Some clients may be resistant to change at first. Just go with the flow. People don't like to feel they are being pushed into making a decision. Show some empathy when this happens. It is easier than arguing with the client. It is the recovery coach's role to support and move when the client is ready.

> Client: *"But I can't quit using. I mean all of my friends use."*
> Coach: *"Oh, I see. So you really couldn't quit using because then you'd be too different to fit in with your friends. Am I hearing that correctly?"*

Exception questions. Exception questions focus on who, what, when and where as they relate to client goals.

- *"Are there times when the problem does not happen or is less serious? When? How does that happen?"*
- *"Have there been times in the last couple of weeks when the problem did not happen or was less severe?"*
- *"How was it that you were able to make this exception happen?"*
- *"What was different about that day?"*
- *"If your friend (teacher, relative, spouse, partner, etc.) were here and I were to ask him what he noticed you doing different on that day, what would he say? What else?"*

Coping questions: Coping questions attempt to help clients shift their focus away from the problem domains and toward what the client is doing to survive the painful or stressful circumstances. They are related in a way to exploring for exceptions.

- *"What have you found that is helpful in managing this situation?"*
- *"Considering how depressed and overwhelmed this makes you feel, how is it that you were able to get out of bed this morning and make it to our appointment (or make it to work)?"*
- *"You say that you're not sure that you can continue working on your goals. What is it that has helped you to work on them up to now?"*

Challenging a client's thinking:
Client: *"I just can't deal with..."*
Coach: *"Okay, but if you could, how would you deal with it?"*
Client: *"I don't know."*
Coach: *"All right, but if you did know, what might that look like?"*

Provoking Extremes:
Coach: *"Okay, suppose you don't change, what then?"*
Client: *"My wife would leave me."*
Coach: *"Would that be devastating? "Are there ways to prevent that from happening?"*

Flashback Questioning
Asking the client to go back in time to the worse moment of their compulsive or addictive behavior: *"Go back to the time you first realized that enough was enough. What were you experiencing that brought you to that realization? Why couldn't you come to that realization the first time you used*, or the second or fifth time? Is reliving that experience worth relapsing?"

Exploring Goals vs. Values

"What do you want out of life?" Ask clients what they consider to be their most important values and then explore how their behavior(s) interfere with reaching those values. Repeat the same process when discussing goals.

Menu Options

"Out of all these potential solutions you have listed, give three you are certain could work." Menu options refer to the identification of several actions clients can take versus one . Emphasis is placed on the client's' willingness to pursue and commit to at least two of the most reasonable/realistic/doable menu actions.

Using the 'Readiness Ruler'

"On a scale from one to ten, ten being the best chance to commit to a change, which number best reflects how ready you are to change?"

Nudging Questions

- *"Are you ready to commit to the next step?"*
- *"You know exactly what needs doing, don't you?"*
- *"Is there anything you need to change about that step?"*
- *"Listen to what you just said. Let's revisit it."*
- *"Sounds like you're waffling. What could you choose to do or not do...I just need to hear a clearer answer."*
- *"What will you do? By when? What will be your next step?"*
- *"What will your life look like by our next meeting if you took just one of those steps?"*

(Sources: Berg, I.K., & Miller, S.D. 1992; The National Center for PTSD; Fredrike Bannink. 2006; Cepeda, L.M. (2006); Bunker, B.B. 2000 Ivey, 2012)

"Honesty with oneself is the first chapter in the book of wisdom."
(Thomas Jefferson)

CHALK TALK

Focused   Questioning Role-Play Exercise

Solicit the help of a partner and create a scenario/dilemma and create your own solutions-focused questions. Remember: <u>you must only use questions.</u> For example:

<u>*Evicting a loved one out of your home for refusing treatment options*</u>
Client: *"I'm having trouble evicting my 26-year old son out of our home until he seeks treatment."*
Coach: *"Can you expand on that a little bit so I can understand it better?" (Clarification)*
Client: *"Well, it has upset the household and my new wife of three years, who is threatening to leave me unless I do something about it."*
Coach: *"So what do you want to see happen?" (Goal identification)*
Client: *"Well, I want my son to enter treatment, but I don't want to upset my relationship with my wife."*
Coach: *"So what steps have you begun to take?" (Coping question)*

(You get the idea. Take a few minutes to play out a questioning scenario of your own with your coaching buddy.)

1. *Clarification question:*

2. *Coping question:*

3. *Challenging question :*

4. *Options question:*

5. *Moving toward action question:*

6. *Next steps questions:*

FOLLOW YOUR CURIOSITY

My doctoral mentor had a saying: *"Judge a person (in this case, coach) by the questions asked not by the answers given."* In this business, there is no greater truth, and there is also no greater expression of commitment that connects more deeply and intensely than *curiosity*. Curiosity is a form of caring in action. It is living proof of your commitment to serve, help and transform. The more authentically curious you are as a coach, the faster your clients will become empowered to work with you and begin making progress.

Curiosity is a magical tool that is loaded with power, and is a large component in solutions-focused questioning. It is important to develop your curiosity if you are going to coach others in making life changes for themselves. When we become curious and ask powerful questions, it gives us a greater and fresher perspectives in our interactions with others. Most clients come to us with just one or two lenses to see the world through, but a curious coach can have many different lenses to view a client's world through. This gives the coach an array of options to explore with his or her client.

Using Solution-Focused Questioning

Solutions-focused questions are an effective way of moving a client towards a solution rather than dwelling on the issues or causes of a problem. Solution-focused questioning is compatible with recovery coaching in that it does not focus on the past, but instead, focuses on the present and helps clients create their own version of a future. It empowers clients to think, analyze, and create answers that will cause them to act.

The coach uses *respectful curiosity* as a method of communicating a feeling of equality in the coaching relationship; a peer, if you will. It invites clients to envision their preferred future and begin exploring options and addressing movement toward a goal. It doesn't matter that these moves may come in small increments. What is important is that exploration is occurring.

To support this process, questions are asked about the client's strengths, their view of the future, and personal or community resources needed to make their vision happen. With guidance from the coach, the client begins to construct that vision of what that future might look like.

Cutting through Defenses

There are times when clients will try to outsmart the coach by diverting the coaching session in different directions, mostly for self-protection. These are common defenses. They are stuck in their own dilemma and will blame other individuals and refuse to take responsibility for their role in causing their dilemma. Don't get caught in that trap. To paraphrase an Albert Ellis quote: *A good [recovery coach] has to have a functioning bull shit detector turned on at all times.* Below are some examples of cutting through a client's defenses.

Taking Responsibility

- ✓ *"What part might you have played in creating this situation?"*
- ✓ *"What do you think needs to be done to take responsibility for this situation?"*
- ✓ *"Since we can't change your (brother, spouse, boss) anyway, let's focus on how you can change and perhaps grow from this."*
- ✓ *"We've talked enough about (your mother-in-law, etc) for quite a while. How about we talk about you?"*
- ✓ *Wait. Let us go back to the original question: what part did you play in this situation?"*
- ✓ *"Tell me how this person really controls your responses."*
- ✓ *"Whoa! Think back for a minute. This is the third time you mentioned____. What is that about?"*

The "Yes, but…" Game

People enjoy playing out the games they learned in childhood. The *"yes, but…"* game always bubbles up in coaching. Never get caught up in this counterproductive game with clients. Remember that the coach has already made an agreement with his or her clients to collaboratively pursue, specific changes that the client desires.

To linger too long on this type of gamesmanship is counter-productive to the growth process. *Yes but-ers* are geniuses at coming up with excuses for inaction. *"Yes, but…"* is always an indirect form of saying *"no,"* or a display of resistance *("I really don't want to do that.")*. It produces obstacles to progress and sucks all the energy from the coaching process.

Instead, practice using the *"yes, and…"* approach with clients. It forces clients to generate better points of view. The "yes and…" paradigm facilitates a continuation of strength-focused dialogue and opens the door to more options and possibilities:

Client: *"Yes, but if I quit I'm afraid I'll be rejected."*
Coach: *"Yes, and…?"*
Client: *"But that would make me hang out alone with no friends."*
Coach: *"Yes, and…?*
Client: *"Well, I would probably be forced to move in with my family."*
Coach: *"Yes, and…"*
Client: *"But that would be pure hell…"*
Coach: *"What do you mean by hell? What is hell for you?"*
Client: *Well, I'm middle aged and I don't see any woman interested in me.*
Coach: *Yes, and that would be hell for you?*
Client: *Oh, yes.*
Coach: *What would be a better way of establishing new relationships if a separation would happen?"*

[One can see how the coaching discussion can go in different directions by virtue of the client's response. There is nothing wrong with that as long as the coach returns to the original dilemma. Again, the coach is strapped in and going along for the ride to wherever the ride leads and merely pointing out the roadblocks and pot holes.

50 SOLUTIONS-FOCUSED QUESTIONS

Below are fifty solution-focused questions that have been effective in recovery coaching:

1. "In a perfect world, what would you like to achieve?"
2. "What do you want to take from this session that can help you?"
3. "Where do you want to go from here?"
4. "If you had the choice of just one miracle, what would it be?"
5. "What would that miracle look like?"
6. "What would be different in your life if you would...?"
7. "How would things look like if your problem was solved?"
8. "What positive things will take the place of the problem?"
9. "How do you think that is a problem for your spouse, friend, others?"
10. "What would you like to see different as a result of ...?"
11. "How will you know when you have reached your goal?"
12. "How would important people (wife, partner, colleagues) in your life know you have reached your goal?"
13. "What would you like to see more of?"
14. "What have you done to make that possible?"
15. "Who would be the people who would know that a change had occurred?"
16. "If you had 24 hours to live, what would you regret not having done?"
17. "What do you see yourself doing differently when your problem has gone away?"
18. "How will you do that exactly?"
19. "How did you know what was needed?"
20. "How is that new for you?"
21. "How has moving from – to – given you hope?"
22. "Suppose you could change as a result of these sessions, what would be different about your life then?"
23. "What has changed since the last session?"
24. "What is better already?"
25. "What were you doing to make things better?"

26. "What do you need to do to assure that your problem happens again in the future?"
27. "What are you doing differently now?"
28. "How did you find the courage to...?"
29. "What gave you the strength to...?"
30. "How did you succeed in doing that?"
31. "What gave you the sense that it was the right time to...?"
32. "When was the last time you had success at...?"
33. "When did you become aware you had those qualities?"
34. "When did other people become aware that you have those qualities?"
35. "In which situations are those qualities most noticeable?"
36. "Name five things that you're doing well and do not need to change?"
37. "How can you do more of the things that do not need to change?"
38. "What is easy for you to do that impresses others?"
39. "If a deceased loved one could see how you live your life now, what would he or she say about you?"
40. "On a scale of 1-10, ten being best, how are you doing?"
41. "Explain what you are doing to increase that score."
42. "What needs to change in order to get you to ten?"
43. "What would a point higher on your scale look like?"
44. "In your opinion, what would a small step forward look like?"
45. "What would be so bad if you...?"
46. "What would be the worst that could happen if...?"
47. "Suppose I am a fly on the wall. What would I see you doing?"
48. "On a scale of 1-10 what are your chances of finding a solution to...?"
49. "How do you plan to achieve that?"
50. "On a scale of one to ten, how ready are you to begin your work?+

(Sources: Excerpted from Fredrike Bannink's 1000 Solution-focused Questions; Tony Stoltzfus: Coaching Questions: A Coaches Guide to Powerful Asking Questions. 1998;Jane Creswell, MCC, 2002.)

NOTES

This module will enable coaches to:

- ➤ Explore the concept of Cognitive Restructuring and the role it plays in recovery coaching.

- ➤ Define Cognitive Distortions in client thinking.

- ➤ Explain and demonstrate the implementation of Cognitive Behavioral Theory (CBT) as used in Cognitive Restructuring.

- ➤ Examine key elements of the A-B-C-D-E Structure of Cognitive Restructuring.

- ➤ Apply Socratic Questioning to challenging cognitive distortions.

HOW ONE THINKS

I always tell clients in recovery, *"Relax. You are not your thoughts."* As was previously noted, the first year abstaining from an addiction is the most difficult. Loss of both control and faulty personal perspectives are not uncommon occurrences in a recovering individual.

During this critical period, several cognitive challenges (doubt, confusion, and irrationality) will occur. If clients successfully identify and deal with these resulting challenges in a logical manner, only then will they be better able to self-manage their lives and maintain stability. This is where Cognitive Restructuring plays an important role in recovery.

Relapse, as does any other compulsive behavior, begins in the brain. Believe it or not, when we talk to ourselves, the brain listens and files all that information away for future use. Cognitive Restructuring explores the notion of rational vs. irrational thinking and is defined as an action-focused process of helping clients challenge their faulty thinking patterns and explore a more balanced or healthier way of processing information.

What is Cognitive Restructuring?

Cognitive Restructuring is learning to identify and dispute irrational or maladaptive thoughts known as cognitive distortions, and is based on the theory that much of how we feel is determined by what we think. This becomes critically important to clients who have graduated from treatment are looking to get their lives back in order, but can't. One reason is that many have been working out of old (but once reliable) life scripts and unreasonable life rules which no longer fit into the sober scheme of things. Regaining a life that was once lost through addictive thinking and behaviors, starts with gaining fresh clarity on values, and stepping back and looking at oneself in the mirror. That is, identifying and challenging our faulty thinking and beliefs. Then it is followed up with structuring a plan that is bolstered with logic and action. Only then can clients begin to create a balanced life for themselves.

You Are Not What You Think

The Foundation for critical thinking (2006) outlines the following important facts about thinking and can be applied to cognitive restructuring:

- ✓ *All thinking has a history in people's lives.*
- ✓ *All thinking is dependent upon a substructure of reason, evidence, and assumptions.*
- ✓ *All thinking leads people in one direction or another.*
- ✓ *All thinking has implications, outcomes and consequences.*

These facts help us highlight the four ways we can help clients come to terms with their faulty thinking: A) We can help clients reflect on how they come to think the way they do on any given issue (family or environmental influences); and B) We can help clients reflect on how they have come to support their thinking and beliefs (assumptions or evidence).

Cognitive restructuring emphasizes rational thinking and healthy behaviors that are more likely to follow accurate, positive, goal-oriented thoughts. The model is comprised of a set of techniques that teach clients to identify their faulty thinking or beliefs and then modifying those that are distorted or are no longer useful in one's sober world. This approach does not involve distorting reality in a positive direction or attempt to believe the unbelievable when it's not. Rather, it is about using reason and evidence to replace distorted thought patterns with more accurate, balanced and functional ones.

Cognitive Restructuring adapts the **A-B-C** principles of Cognitive Behavioral Therapy (CBT) pioneered by Drs. Albert Ellis and Aaron Beck. CBT holds that most of our emotions and behaviors are the result of how we interpret events that activate anger and self-doubt **(A)** in the social environment in which we interact. These events shape how one feels or believes **(B)** and helps determine how one will respond to people and events. The consequences can be positive or negative **(C)** but people with cognitive disorders, the consequences are usually negative, often because our interpretations and underlying thoughts and beliefs contain errors in thinking which while addicted, may have had short term benefits, but sober, are not very useful nor helpful to clients recovery. This results in unnecessary suffering and often causes us to react in ways that are not always in our best interest. Mental health practitioners commonly refer to this as having *cognitive distortions* while the A.A. folks call it *stinky thinking*. Recovery coaches just call it *negative mindsets.*

ORIGINS AND FUNCTION OF COGNITIVE DISTORTIONS

Cognitive distortions, a term coined by researcher David Beck and later popularized by A.A. as *"stinky thinking"* is defined as: *reoccurring, exaggerated or irrational thought patterns that are believed to perpetuate the effects of doubt, guilt, anxiety and depression.* In coaching we simply call that *erroneous thinking or beliefs*. Most, if not all, recovering persons have cognitive distortions which may include: *Jumping to conclusions, rationalizing, minimizing, "shoulda, woulda, coulda"* thinking, and *catastrophizing* to name a few.

Many clients who are discharged from treatment come to coaching still somewhat confused and uncertain about their recovery future. And their negative mindsets have caused them problems in the past and are often revisited in aftercare. Moreover, these reoccurring maladaptive thoughts may continue to reinforce negative thinking or emotions; convincing themselves that their view of the world must be rational and accurate, when in fact it's not. These faulty beliefs will continue to make their lives even more miserable even in recovery coaching. By correcting these inaccurate beliefs, and replacing them with more rational and balanced thoughts, the client's perception of events and emotional state can begin to improve. This is done through teaching, coaching and practicing new thoughts and behaviors through a supportive and trusting coach-client relationship. *(Grohol, J. (2009). 15 Common Cognitive Distortions. David Beck. (1972). Depression: Causes and Treatment. 1984. L.D. Gonzales, 2001.)*

Self-Limiting Thinking

Some cognitive distortions may have a grain of thought in them, but for the most part are not very accurate: *"That's what I've been taught and I expect the same from my children."* The more a person's thinking is characterized by these distortions, the more they are likely to experience disturbing emotions or engage in maladaptive behaviors.

The literature points to past programming and childhood developmental experiences as two of the main causes of cognitive distortions. Learned short-cut habits and observations of how parents, peers, or significant others viewed and coped with difficult life experiences, often justified inaction or protection from possible failure. These shortcut solutions were sought and practiced until they became a part of one's go-to, default mechanism. People under great pressure or stress are more apt to take cognitive shortcuts resulting in less accurate, more distorted interpretations of reality. These self-limiting thoughts keep people stuck in old patterns that don't always work to their benefit. In recovery coaching, these patterns are called addictive thinking behaviors or habits and are the very thing a coach helps and supports clients in identifying and challenging.

Identifying Cognitive Distortions

Remember that the first crucial months of recovery are usually the most difficult for clients. They may not be in full control of things happening around them and need help in learning how to change the way they think and react to the excessive stimulus pouring out of the sober world. They are mired in what addiction experts refer to as addictive thinking: protective defensiveness, denial, etc. This is totally different from logical thinkers who use effective processing skills and coping plans to process information.

When pressured, the recovering client will tend to build a case around self-defeating conclusions or desired outcomes, whether they are logical or not, and whether or not the facts support it: *"The pressure is too strong so I must take something to stabilize."* Recovery coaches refer to this phenomenon as being in a *distorted thinking* mode. Over the using months or years, these cognitive distortions have become automatic and reliable tools to the using client and have become helpful in risk-avoidance, taking action or not taking responsibility for their behaviors. Fresh out of treatment, cognitive distortions usually go unchallenged, unresolved and may still linger in a client's mind. Some distortions may hold a grain of truth, but for the most part they are inaccurate, sometimes toxic, but certainly not useful in a person's recovery process.

Challenging them can be like opening a fresh wound and tends to generate the same uncomfortable or negative feelings, self-defeating urges and actions of the past: fear, hostility, shame and ultimately, relapse. As recovery coaches it becomes crucial that we proceed slowly and carefully when exposing cognitive distortions.

Below are a series of cognitive distortions or negative mindsets which almost always invite frustration and anger in people. Although some negative automatic thoughts may be true, most are either untrue or have only a grain of truth in them:

All-or-Nothing

Thinking that things are black or white, never grey, e.g., if your performance falls short of perfect, you see yourself as a total failure.

Overgeneralization

Seeing a single, negative event as a never-ending pattern, e.g. *"I'm always messing things up. I never get anything right. I might as well give up, I'll only relapse again."*

Perfectionist

Having rigid rules for self-guidance, must-thinking or having a precise, fixed idea of how one or others should behave, and overestimating how bad it is when these expectations are not met: "I must do this because that is the way I was raised." Or, "My kids must do this, because that is what I was taught."

Personalization & Self Blamers

Holding oneself personally responsible for events that aren't (or aren't entirely) under one's control: "It's my fault that we didn't get to the concert on time. I always screw things up." The self-blamer always winds up taking all the hits, but getting a sick payoff from wallowing in the guilt that's generated.

Disqualifying the Positive

Rejecting positive experiences by insisting that they don't count or they weren't earned anyway. In this, the person continues to see everything as negative even when their everyday experiences contradict this: "Sure, I was just lucky this time."

Jumping to Conclusions

Making negative interpretations even though there are no definite facts that convincingly support the interpretation.

Mind Reading

Thinking that someone is reacting negatively to you and no effort is made to fact-check it.

The Fortune-Teller

Always anticipating things will turn out badly and that the prediction is an already established fact. "Why bother, I'll only spoil the event anyway."

Magnifying or Minimizing

When the importance of things is exaggerated or minimized. This happens when a serious error happens, but a claim is made, "It's no big thing," or "It wasn't meant to be," but the person continues to feel guilty about it anyway.

Emotional Reasoning

The belief that our negative emotions reflect the way things really are: "I feel it, therefore it must be."

"Should, Must, Ought To" Statements

This is when people try to motivate themselves with a series of *should* and *should-nots*, as if they have to feel whipped and punished before they can be expected to do anything. The emotional consequences are feelings of guilt and inadequacy. When we tell others they *should* or *must* do something and they don't follow through, our first response is feelings of disappointment, frustration and resentment: "I should (must) do this or my kids (or significant other) won't like me."

Overgeneralization

Making sweeping negative conclusions that go far beyond the real or current situation, "I really blew the interview. I don't have what it takes to succeed in that position anyway."

(Sources: Challenges, Inc. 1998. Berg, J.S. Cognitive Therapy Basics.1996. The Beck Institute, 2003. David Burns: The Revolution of Thought, 1998. Nelson Binggeli: CBT Techniques, 2009. David Burns: The Feeling Good Handbook, 1999.)

Function of Cognitive Restructuring

Cognitive work that occurs immediately after treatment can be easily learned and practiced, and the benefits will continue throughout a client's recovery process and may even improve other areas in life which may not be even be related to the addiction.

Cognitive restructuring is not to be interpreted as a branch of positive thinking. It is more accurate to say that cognitive restructuring is more about creating balanced or realistic thinking. The primary function of cognitive restructuring is helping clients put things in their proper perspective by teaching them to recognize and dispute any distortions or irrational thinking habits and replacing them with more neutral, accurate or rational ones. Cognitive restructuring has three basic steps:

1. Identifying the thoughts or beliefs that are influencing the disturbing emotion;
2. Evaluating those thoughts and beliefs for their accuracy and usefulness using logic and evidence; and
3. Modifying or replacing those thoughts or beliefs with ones that are more accurate, balanced, neutral or useful.

Through a process of questioning, and the application of reasoning and logic, you are supporting the client in stepping back and taking a hard look at any cognitive gaps in their thinking and beliefs. As their realities become clearer, clients can better perceive themselves and the world as it relates to maintaining a sober lifestyle.

The A-B-C's OF COGNITIVE RESTRUCTURING

The approach to Cognitive Restructuring (CR) has been formulated in a basic A-B-C structure outlined in the Cognitive Behavior Therapy (CBT) literature, developed by Albert Ellis and Aaron Beck, and is based on the theory that all stressful states are a result of, and often maintained by biased, distorted or irrational ways of thinking and believing which manifest themselves automatically in the recovering person's mind.

These automatic thoughts have been rehearsed and practiced so many times in the life of a client that they have now become habitual and ingrained in the lowest level of conscious awareness. They are irrational because it makes a person feel bad and causes them to do things that make their situation painfully worse, not better. The recovery coach's role then is to help clients identify and challenge their irrational beliefs or faulty thinking habits and support them in their restructuring those cognitive distortions through a system of evidence and logic.

It is important to note that CR doesn't focus on how clients' pessimistic thoughts came about or the underlying issues that brought about such thoughts. CR's aim is to help clients extinguish those distressing thoughts and create newer, more neutral or positive ones that can create change. The first step in the recovery process is to focus on introducing clients to the A-B-C components of emotional distress as described below.

The A-B-C's of Cognitive Restructuring:

A) <u>Adversity event</u>: Something happened; a self-defeating thought occurred, something was said, or an actual event has occurred " This is the second time I've been excluded from the meeting."

B) <u>Belief system</u>: Consists of automatic, irrational thoughts and beliefs that may result from the event (A) above: I'm hopeless; I'm a failure.

C) <u>Consequence:</u> Describes the actions or reactions a person takes as a result of the event(s) that occurred in A (above) as interpreted at B. (depression, aggression, isolation, chronic absenteeism).

Challenging Faulty Thinking

Once clients are taught to understand Ellis' A-B-C behavioral theory, the recovery coach can introduce the last 2 steps used in cognitive restructuring, D and E:

"D" is the disputing or challenging of contradicting statements we make and cognitive options available that can result in more balanced and rational thinking.

> D) <u>Disputing our beliefs</u>: This is the *"Says who!"* section of cognitive restructuring where clients are guided through a process of self-talk and cost-benefit analysis to dispute their maladaptive thoughts and their faulty belief system discussed in (B) above: "Says who? Where is the evidence that says I'm a loser? Is my thinking logical? Is it true? What is so awful about this?" This is also where clients are taught to explore better options and rational alternatives. Below are a few illustrations:
>
> 1. *Fact-checking.* Approaching the person who created the adverse event at (A) and fact-checking motives. Maybe it was an oversight or not pertinent to you department or expertise or they just plain forgot to alert you about the meeting.

2. *Self-talk it through.* "Am I really a loser? Says who?"
   Based on the conclusions made in D, clients can begin the
   process of self-talk that can re-program their thinking that can
   lead to new, self-empowering behaviors. A recovery coach uses
   cognitive restructuring techniques to encourage clients to
   explore counter examples to the claims being made in B above
   (I'm a loser), and if there are ways to moderate that claim ("*Yes, I
   make mistakes now and then, but I'm learning from them, and
   that doesn't make me a loser.*").

"E" is the execution of a neutral or positive plan of action that focuses
on the positive or constructive aspects of a problematic situation or
experience. Executing a workable plan can lead to more positive
emotions which lead to more rational ways of addressing challenges or
problems. The execution of a "better" plan can be done through the
process of applying of logic and reason, solution-focused questioning
or through Self-Talk Analysis: *"Who owns this problem anyway?"* or
"What are my options here?" and *"Where is the proof that says..."*

Guided Discovery in challenging distortions

"Don't believe everything you think", is a common phrase in cognitive
restructuring. Guided discovery is probably one of the best questioning tools
used in challenging faulty automatic thinking patterns. Using an optometry
analogy, of coaching clients through stages *D* and *E* of cognitive restructuring
is like getting your eyes checked. The optician places a range of lenses in front
of your eyes. At first all you see is a blur, but through the process of adjusting
and feedback from the client, the blur soon goes away and your vision
becomes clearer. The same can be said of guided discovery except that
through questioning, the coach is processing information through lens' of
perceptions, if you will, thus allowing the client to access a range of
choices/options. It is a quick and effect way of processing information in
different ways, ostensibly, to see their life through different perspectives and
allowing our emotional reaction to events in life to shift. In recovery coaching,

these types of continued conscious re-evaluations are very important because they lay the foundation for building future automatic thinking habits that are more helpful and make a relapse less likely.

Modifying faulty thinking makes clients feel more motivated to continue on the road of recovery knowing that they have the proper tools to question their erroneous beliefs when adversity raises its ugly head. Finally, it is helpful to remember that it may have taken a lifetime to develop these patterns of thought, and it will take time and hard work to change them. Below are examples of questions that can be used in Guided Discovery when challenging clients' irrational thinking and beliefs.

Lens' of perception

"How reliable is the evidence supporting (or refuting) your beliefs?"
"Do you think that other people consider your evidence convincing? Irrational? A little extreme?"
"What would be the worst that could happen if…?"
"Could you convince a jury that your statement is true?"
"What could be some of the errors in your thinking?"
"How did you arrive at your conclusions?"
"What is the best alternative in changing this situation?"
"Just because one or two people have said it, does that make it true?"
"Are there others that think you're….? (Two clowns don't make a circus.)"
"What is your definition of failure, acceptance, success, worthlessness?"
"What other choices do you have? What are your options?"

Options Questions

Option questions are designed to help clients think creatively in developing potential solutions. An effective coach always lets the client do all the heavy lifting in thinking things through instead of offering solutions and suggestions. Some option questions include:
"What could you begin doing about this problem?"
"Who do you know that could help you…?"
"What other resources do you have that could help you…?"
"What have you seen others do that may work for you?"

Checking for Motivation

It is always good to assess a client's readiness to move forward on a plan:
"On a scale of one to ten, how likely is it that you will...?"
"How can you modify that step to move it from a six to a ten?"
"Are there any obstacles we still need to address in order to...?"

Looking At All the Angles

"Let's turn that into an action step: what will you do by next month?"
"Which of these three options look doable for next week?"
"You mentioned that you could do_____. What will you commit to doing?"
"What are the pros and cons in pursuing the option you have selected?"
"What is your gut telling you at this moment?"
"What is the big payoff in making this decision?"

Perspectives Questions

- ✓ "For the sake of argument, let's assume you had the power to change your...
- ✓ "How do you see yourself *in control* rather than *controlled?*"
- ✓ "Just what is motivating you to move in this direction?"
- ✓ "Let's look at a couple of motives and options here. If you were to change that situation, what would it look like?"
- ✓ "Which option of those three will require stretching out a bit?"

The Restructuring Process

Cognitive restructuring refers to the process of replacing distorted thinking with thoughts that are more accurate and useful. We have learned that cognitive restructuring has three basic steps: (1) Identifying the thoughts or beliefs that are influencing the disturbing emotion(s); (2) Evaluating them for their accuracy and usefulness using logic and evidence; and 3) modifying or replacing the thoughts with ones that are more accurate, neutral or useful. It is about supporting clients develop more balanced or realistic thinking habits, to put things in their proper perspective and construct more rational plans that can help them transition and self-manage their lives in their new, sober environment without having to rely on substances.

Cognitive Restructuring Techniques

1. **Modeling:** Conducting role playing exercises.

2. **Cognitive Rehearsal:** Coach asks client to rehearse positive outcomes or thoughts.

3. **Validity Testing:** Weighing the pros and cons and offer objective evidence.

4. **Journaling:** Maintaining a journal or diary.

5. **Homework**: Set of practical assignments to be completed by client such as practicing new techniques, listening to audio tapes, reading articles and books.

6. **Metaphors:** The use of metaphors (like the one in 5 above) to break through distortions. A coach uses metaphors to simplify a complex issue or thought.

(Sources: F. Rosiellio, Ph.D.; J Manning, Ph.D.; L.D. Gonzales Ph.D.; www.cbtworkshops.com)

Top Five Mistakes Coaches Make in Cognitive Restructuring

1. Asking closed questions – avoid asking questions that can be answered with a simple "yes" or "no". There are coaches who prefer to take the easy route by asking questions that can quickly serve the coaches agenda (moving forward, ending on time, etc). Instead convert (or restate) close questions to open ones: *"Can you list two ways you can do that and still keep evenings open for family?"* or *"Interesting, is there another way to approach that?"*

2. Rambling questions: When I first began coaching I was guilty of asking the same question three different ways, thus confusing the client as to which question to answer first. I did this because I wasn't really sure of the question I wanted to ask so with sweaty palms and parched lips I would "shotgun" my clients with three or four questions in a row. Stop! Don't do what I did. Think, and formulate your question before asking it. It's okay to pause and think. Just trust the coaching process and stop

looking for the (Holy Grail) of perfect questions. They don't exist. You just want whatever is going to help the client move along. A good continuation question could be, *"You mentioned earlier that___. Tell me more about that."* In coaching always use connecting leaders such as: *"What's going on here...,* *"Expand on that."* or *"Tell me more."*

3. Refusing to interrupt where appropriate. That's right. This is not a misprint. One of your jobs as a coach is to manage the coaching process, so when you see a client bird-hopping all over the place, it is perfectly appropriate to interrupt and bring things back into focus.

4. Rhetorical questioning: Although formed with the client's interest at heart, this type of questioning can often be biased, emotional, and judgmental and often based on your own personal opinion. Always eliminate rhetorical questioning from your coaching style as this is a good indicator of personal bias towards the client. Some examples of rhetorical questioning include:

   a. *"What were you thinking!?*

   b. *"Really. Is that a cop out?*

   c. *"Are you willing to throw you marriage away for...?"*

5. *Why* questions: Avoid asking "why" questions. Why questions only make clients clam up and want to protect themselves from exposure, and they force clients to want to justify or defend their position. Coaches do better with "what" questions:

   a. Change *"Why did you...? To "What led you to...?"*

   b. Change *"Why can't you just talk to him about...?"* to *"What do you need to talk to him about that could change...?"*

   c. Change *"Why are you feeling down about..."* to *"What is causing you to feel..."*

CHALK TALK

Change each problem-focused question to solutions-focused questions using the examples previously provided.

- "What is the problem?" to _____

- What is hindering you?" to _____

- "What is the main issue?" to _____

- How long have you been experiencing this problem?" to_____
  _____

- "Who do you think is to blame?" to_____

- "Could you be the cause of the problem?" to_____

Exercise: With your coaching buddy, make up & practice converting problem-focused questions to solutions-focused questions by each of you asking a series of questions and then reversing the process.

1. _____to _____.
2. _____to_____.
3. _____to_____.
4. _____ to _____.
5. _____ to _____.

THE USE OF METAPHORS IN COACHING

I have often been accused of talking in parables and metaphors because the use of metaphors is useful in making seemingly sophisticated concepts easier to understand by clients in transition. As you already know, clients in aftercare often suffer from lingering cognitive distortions and sometimes the use of metaphors can be very helpful in understanding and challenging their faulty thinking. It's kind of like spraying WD-40 in their brain and loosening those rusty gears (metaphor?).

The beauty of metaphors is that they are simple to use. They can be a paragraph long or just a one-liner. Metaphors do not have to be clever, dramatic or sophisticated. But when used properly, they can tap into clients' pre-existing knowledge and familiar understanding of a problem that on the surface seemed complex and complicated, but has now been reduced from psycho-babble to easily understood, visual terms. The understanding of a problem through the use of metaphors, options or solutions can be easily transferred to new and fresh views and a client's motivation to explore a variety of options is enhanced.

Below are a few examples of metaphors I have borrowed and used when coaching across all ages:

1. **About building awareness**

   Imagine a very poor mineral prospector living in a little shanty out in the hills. The only thing he owns in the world is his shanty. What he does not know is that just beneath his shanty, hidden in the dirt, is an inexhaustible vein of gold. As long as he remains ignorant of his hidden wealth, this miner will remain in poverty; but when he focuses more on his own dwelling and its surroundings, he is bound to discover his own fathomless wealth. (Discuss about being observant of the world around us.)

2. About getting to the source of a problem

Problems and issues are like weeds in a garden. The weeds are our automatic thoughts, assumptions we make, and the roots are our ingrained beliefs. As the weeds grow, we can pull out our weed-whacker and cut them down, and we're good for a while until two weeks later when the weeds come up again. Then you repeat the same ritual. There is another option. You can dig down deep (core beliefs) and dig up the roots once and for all. If you don't deal with the roots (your beliefs), the roots (reoccurring thoughts and attitudes) will just keep growing back.

3. About exposure to something beneficial

Learning the skills I will teach you is very much like an oyster protecting itself from an irritant. When a grain of sand gets inside the oyster it becomes an irritant to the oyster. The oyster then protects itself by encasing that grain of sand with a protective coating thus providing relief from all that irritation and pain. The result is a beautiful pearl. Similarly, life may have become a great irritant to you, but the skills you will learn in this (class, program) will help you develop something valuable for your current discomfort. You will feel better about yourself and will continue to have value in your life long after your original problems are gone.

4. Expressing empathy

I understand you may be as nervous as a cat in a room full of rocking chairs. Okay, *based on what you just told me about your schedule,* it sounds as if you're being steamrolled into something you don't want to do. Follow-up with: *"Who is the steamroller? Who are you in this scenario?...Is there a way you could turn away from that steamroller or at least slow it down?... How* would that look?" Or, *"It sounds to me like you were trying to stuff a square peg into a round whole...am I correct?"* Or, *"Sometimes it seems like you're rolling the dice and crapping out."*

5. Cleaning out the closest (Letting go)

Imagine your life as a closet where you randomly put the things you don't want with the things you want to keep. Suddenly you find yourself putting in more things that you don't want to keep until one day you open the door and everything unwanted comes flying out. Everything will remain messy and cluttered until you have a spring cleaning. Our minds are often like that. We pack in unwanted thoughts until we come to a point where we just can't focus or think anymore. Our mind gets so cluttered to the point that we have to get rid of what we don't want or is preventing us from getting to what we do want.

6. **Explaining the Process of Change**

Change is not orderly or progressive. It's sudden, explosive, and unexpected. It's more like trying to get ketchup out of a bottle. You grasp the ketchup bottle tightly and you shake it, but nothing comes out. You shake it again and still nothing happens. Then you apply more effort until finally you give it one more shake and SPLAT! There's ketchup all over your fries.

7. **Everyone Matters**

One day, I was jogging on the beach and far up ahead I saw a figure of a man throwing something into the ocean. When I reached him I noticed that he was throwing back starfish that had washed ashore and were now beginning to dry up from the warm sunshine. I asked him, "Why are you putting these starfish back in the ocean when there are hundreds lying out here in the sand? Why should it matter?" The man quietly picked up another starfish and quietly mumbled, "It matters to this one."

8. *The Wizard of Oz Scenario*

People are always looking for magical solutions somewhere outside ones self. The three characters (lion, tin man, and scarecrow) are good examples. Often we already have the answers within us and just have to tap into them. For others, it takes a Wizard (A recovery coach?) to tease those great qualities out.

9. **Time is Money**

Time is money: yesterday is a cancelled check; tomorrow is a promissory note. Today is the only cash you have, so spend it wisely.

10. **Change Your Strategy**

I walk down the street and there is a deep hole in the sidewalk. I fall in and it takes a long time to get out. I walk down the same street and that deep hole is still there. I pretend not to see it, so I fall in again. I can't believe I'm in the same hole. It takes me a long time to get out. I walk down the same street, but I try to avoid the big hole, and I fall in anyway. I knew I would fall in, but it's a habit. I've been here before, so I quickly get out.
I walk down the same street and I see that big hole. This time I walk around it, but I know someday I could forget and fall in again.
Today, I have decided to walk down a different street.

11. **The Mind as a Computer (for youth)**

The mind is like a computer where the drug of choice has contaminated the brain much like viruses contaminate a computer whereby neither can function properly and ultimately crash. Similarly, when the frontal cortex of the brain that controls rational thinking becomes saturated with drugs or alcohol, it becomes greatly altered and rational thinking becomes limited or is no longer possible. Once the metaphor is understood, the helping person can launch into more sophisticated concepts and interpretations of the addiction process.

12. **About Choices**

"You can either be a passenger on the bus or you can be the driver and determine where you want the bus to go". Or, "Do you want to be the one doing the getting or the one getting done?" Or, "Who's rowing this boat, you or…?" Or, "On life's barge you can either be the fisherman or the guy that cuts bait. Where do you see yourself?"

13. **Making an Omelet**

"In order to make an omelet you have to break a few eggs," means that you can break an egg or two, but breaking a few eggs is not enough. and a critical meaning that you have to make some sacrifices, a critical point in recovery. In recovery coaching we use this metaphor to launch into discussions relating to a readiness to consider next-step thinking and ultimately, change.

14. **Life on a Fish hook**

Life on a fish hook is a metaphor about forgiveness. Being unforgiving is like being on a giant fishhook. On the same hook hangs the person that hurt you. The hook is extremely painful and wherever you go the hook goes with you and so does the person who offended you. The only way you can get yourself off the hook is if you allow the other person off first. The cost of not allowing the person that hurt you to get off the hook first is, perhaps can bring a lifetime of unhappiness."

15. **Alice In Wonderland-Going in any direction is not movement**

In the Lewis Carroll novel Alice asked the Cheshire cat for directions when she became lost. Alice: *"Which direction shall I go?"* The cat replied, *"Well, that depends where you're going."* Alice: *"But I don't know where I'm going."* Cat: *"Then it doesn't matter which direction you go."* Going in any direction without a plan or a roadmap can be counter-productive and comes with a high cost in our recovery journey.

It is important to note that metaphors, though useful tools when trying to convey and idea or point in the coaching process, should always be used sparingly as they tend to lose their effectiveness when frequently used.

(Creative sources: Mike T. Lanjo MSW; Eleanor Avinor, Ph.D.; Portia Nelson; True Recovery Coaching; Ray Mathis, MSW; Beth Ross, Ph.D.; Lisa Fierro, RPN; and, of course, my grandmother.)

NOTES

MODULE EIGHT
Self-Talk Analysis

This module will enable coaches to:

➢ Explore the concept of self-talk analysis in self-coaching.

➢ Delineate the benefits of positive self-talk when used in cognitive restructuring.

➢ Examine key self-talk techniques and how the concept helps clients become their own rescuers.

WE ARE NOT WHAT WE THINK

I once heard a motivational speaker say, *"It's not who we are that holds us back, it's who we think we're not."* All coaches help clients unveil their own nature, and empower them to uncover inexhaustible sources of self-wisdom and power. Like the Wizard of Oz might have told the tin man, scarecrow and the lion, *"It is nothing you need to acquire, from anywhere or anyone. It has always been there inside you. All you need to do is unveil it."*

Self-talk analysis then, like the Wizard, places clients in a position to become their own rescuers. Although Albert Ellis (of RET fame) and Aaron Beck are given credit for self-talk therapy, it began with the Buddha: *"We are what we think, and all that we are arises from our thoughts."*

Self-talk draws on the simple idea that what we say to ourselves the brain listens and files it away for future use. This almost always signals how we are going to feel about or react to an external stimulus or event. The technique provides relatively quick results and places clients in an active role in their own recovery which is the aim of recovery coaching. Self-talk is well-accepted because it makes good common sense; it is non-intrusive and can be done alone. It is based on the belief that when we say something to ourselves, the brain listens and files it away for future reference. This is referred to in the behavioral sciences as Neuro-Linguistic Programming (NLP), but for purposes of cognitive restructuring, the term means self-programming or as my students say, *"Psyching yourself out."*

How we think about a situation or event will determine our feelings and emotions and later, our behaviors and actions. In early addiction recovery, clients' thoughts are often not in line with how 98% of the sober population views the world; the remaining two percent are living in an alternative reality. This is the cognitive dissonance concept previously discussed.

Self-talk can be either productive or self-sabotaging, but in each case follows a specific sequence of steps:

1) The stimulus (which triggers an emotion).
2) Self-talk or inner dialogue to determine what the stimulus means.
3) Emotion/reaction or a consequence that occurs as a result of the self-talk.

The content of our self-talk will almost always decide how we feel or react to an event or a comment made by someone. When we give ourselves repeated negative messages about events and comments we tend to lose control and set ourselves up as victims. Illustrative examples include:

- ✓ Pessimistic about the future.
- ✓ Bitterness about the past.
- ✓ Overly critical of own behavior.
- ✓ Resenting other (sober) people.
- ✓ Feeling they are worse off than anyone else.
- ✓ Inner voice finds reason to criticize.

Consequences of Negative Self-talk

- Self-doubt
- Anxiety
- Symptoms of depression
- Unable to make maintain meaningful relationships.
- Little or no gain of serenity/inner peace
- Urges to pick up the addiction…relapse.

Benefits of Self-talk

Self-talk is the most inexpensive form of self-therapy. Self-talk enables us to use our own innate abilities to manage and control our lives. Self-talk is rewarding in a number of other ways. It gives you ample opportunity to become self-reliant, enhances your self-esteem and confidence in yourself. Through this technique, you will be able to learn more about yourself and appreciate yourself for who you are. Self-talk leads to self-awareness, something that is vital for your success in life. During self-talk, people can sometimes find answers to mind-boggling problems. The person expresses everything that emerges from his or her subconscious, and, more often than not, comes up with valuable information and answers to many of life's problems.

Challenging Our Distorted Thoughts

Below are ten self-talk questions that can be used when challenging unrealistic expectations and dispute irrational thinking:

"What is really going on here?"

"Who owns this problem?"

"How important is the big picture?"

"Who or what else is involved in this problem?"

"Is my interpretation of this thought based on objective reality?"

"Are these thoughts helping me to reach my long- and short-term goals?"

"Are these thoughts helping me to protect my life and my health?"

"What are the costs of thinking this way? What are the benefits?"

"Are these thoughts helping me to feel the way I really want to feel?"

"Are these thoughts helping me to appropriately interact with those who are important to me?"

 **Applying Self-Talk (exercise)**

With your coaching buddy, create a scenario of what things look like to you and practice what things would look like from your coaching buddy's point of view. Insert the techniques previously mentioned to establish your perspectives. Explore barriers, options, and possible solutions. The person that plays "coach" must only use questions. Remember: You are what you practice.

Practice Dilemma: Starting your own coaching business

Response(s)

_____
_____
_____
_____

Your Own Dilemma:

_____
_____
_____
_____

Response(s):

_____
_____
_____
_____

NOTES

MODULE NINE
ANGER AVOIDANCE
IN RECOVERY

This module will enable coaches to:

- ➢ Understand and explain how the principles of anger differ when applied to recovering individuals.

- ➢ Understand and describe the anger feelings generated by functioning in the sober world.

- ➢ Recognize and discuss basic anger signs.

- ➢ Outline basic alternatives to anger.

MANAGING ANGER IN RECOVERY

Anger management? Yes, I know that's an old school term, but is still useful in today's work with recovering clients, indeed everyone. But because there are clients who may have never properly addressed or adjusted to anger issues related to their addictions, teaching them how to manage anger can be like teaching a child how to handle nitroglycerin. That said, a disclaimer may be in order at this point: *The information provided by Starting Point in this module is general, and should not be taken as specific to any individual or circumstance. You should evaluate any of the information provided for your professional own use. Coaching others through anger control and management can be a risky business and is important to note that a recovery coach, may need refer from time-to-time any overt displays of anger or frustration in clients to an appropriately trained professional for help or cease to provide services altogether.*

Because anger is associated with aggression and violence, and because relatively few of us grew up with a healthy model of how to handle angry feelings which is probably why so many people avoid anger at any cost. Heaven forbid someone should get angry! Anger is scary for most Americans, worse for those in recovery. That is why I felt compelled to place the disclaimer in the first paragraph. Coaching persons recovery or recently released from incarceration for drug-related crimes can often get a bit dicey to say the least.

Anger 101

It doesn't hurt to remind clients (and ourselves) that anger is an emotion. Like any other emotion (love, hate, joy), it is neither good nor bad. It is just that, an emotion and something that was learned early in life as: 1) a way of coping with pain; 2) as a temporary way of dealing with fear, helplessness, and lack of control; and 3) a trusted habit that regardless of the pain it causes, one is not able break away from. It's perfectly healthy and normal to feel angry when you've been wronged. But the feeling isn't the problem—it's what you do with it that makes a difference. Anger becomes a problem when it becomes chronic and harms you or others.

Anger is also energy. Too much of it can be bad. If managed incorrectly, anger can have expensive and sometimes deadly consequences. Chronic anger can have serious consequences during one's most critical times of stress where frustrations are popping out of the woodwork like the pop-ups on our computer. These anger outbursts can have an effect on our relationships, our health, our state of mind, and, if one is in recovery for addictive disorders, anger can diminish our chances of a successful recovery.

The good news is that teaching clients how to get their anger under control may be easier than they might think. With a coaching and insight into the real reasons for their anger and some effective tools that can be used in dealing with anger, clients can learn how to express their feelings in healthier ways, thus preventing their temper from hijacking their lives.

My approach with anger management when working with recovering clients is to work collaboratively on explaining the potential causes of anger and helping clients changing the way we think that created their feelings of anger. I tend to lean heavily on the teachings of Aaron Beck, Albert Bandura who have taught that it doesn't matter health-wise whether people let their anger out or keep it in. At the end of the day, the healthiest person is the one who doesn't let things upset them so that they don't get angry in the first place. In my work with recovering teens and adults, I've tried to address the issues of drug dependency and anger simultaneously. That is, it's always better to avoid anger situations up front so that you don't have to manage them through the use of addictive substances. The cognitive restructuring research also suggests that people do not become upset by others' behaviors so much as they become upset themselves through the cognitive choices they make while responding to other people's behaviors or events (re-visit module seven: CBT/cognitive restructuring). It's our thoughts about what was done or said and our interpretation of those events that make us angry and upset such as: arriving at the wrong conclusions, making unreasonable demands of ourselves and others, and having to deal with failed expectations, for example.

The Man in the Mirror

When it comes to managing anger men differ from women. I focus on men because this group is most typically referred to anger management services. Without going into great detail, it has been shown that anger produces a physiological arousal (a surge of adrenaline) in men by creating a state of readiness and a heightened awareness. Blame it if you wish on the *fight* or *flight* learned responses left over from prehistoric days which manifested in some form of protection or aggression. Studies show that unlike most women, men are not very skilled at understanding their emotions and are very uncomfortable when dealing with them. That is why many men prefer to keep a tight lid on their emotions.

What do many men do when they hit their thumb with a hammer? They get angry instead of crying because that is what they have been taught a man is supposed to do. Most men also get angry when faced with an emotional crisis, especially with issues relating to separation. Psychologists call this *abandonment rage.* Again, this is a protective mechanism for their fragile egos; egos that may be covering secretly ingrained feelings of inadequacy or incompetence. So, they respond in the only way they know which is to lash out. And that is why a disproportionate number of men attend anger management classes often when it is too late.

Most Common Types of Anger

Behavioral Anger - This is the most dangerous form of anger and usually describes someone who is physically aggressive towards whatever or whoever triggered their anger (aka: physical abuse).

Verbal Anger - Anger that's expressed mostly through words, actions. Tossing out "F" bombs like rice at a wedding when criticizing and insulting people (aka: verbal abuse).

Paranoid Anger – This anger involves real or imagined jealousy towards others, because they feel other people have or want to take what's rightfully theirs. Or they may act out because they feel intimidated by others (aka: the jealous wife/husband syndrome).

Passive-Aggressive Anger – Sarcasm or mockery is commonly used as a way to hide one's feelings and is expressed to cover up some form of anger. It is usually intended to avoid confrontations with people or situations.

Judgmental Anger – Putting other people down and making them feel bad about themselves, or abilities. This person expresses their feelings by making those around them feel worthless.

And the list goes on, but you get the picture. These are the most common kinds of anger and teaching recovery clients on identifying them is one of the first steps to mastering their anger.

The Connection between Recovery and Anger

Studies have also shown *(T. Gorski, T. Harbin, et al)* that unaddressed anger in recovery is the most powerful relapse trigger. Avoiding anger-invoking situations which can trigger anger and notions to relapse can be a bit more challenging with clients in recovery just by the mere virtue of having to cope in a sober world. Many recovering clients have a tendency to come to us in recovery with anger issues they never had before addiction and not fully understanding why. They can't see the connection between anger and recovery or have not been taught to express anger in healthy ways or how to confront life's challenges in productive, non-violent ways.

People who are recovering from addictive disorders deal with anger issues in more deeper and overt ways. They may deal with recovery anger issues in one of the following ways:

- They may become overly aggressive, and use verbal and physical methods to get out their frustrations.
- They vent or express dislike for people who don't empathize with their recovery challenges.
- They avoid or don't know how to explore the source(s) of their anger.

Because of a lack of learned coping skills, many clients may have become so cut off from their anger that they render themselves as victims. Clients must be taught that anger and substance dependency are first cousins, plain and simple and because there is seldom enough time to address them simultaneously in treatment, they need to be addressed in aftercare.

To begin with, there are both internal and external barriers occurring all at once in a recovering person's life. Imagine for one moment coming out of a residential treatment facility or jail and having to face job loss, unable to qualify for housing, loss of financial aid for college, and a probation officer looking over your shoulder as you conduct a U.A. *(Urine Analysis)* just to prove that you're clean. Now also, imagine a demanding spouse with a laundry list of to-do's and ordering, *"Well, now that you're home and sober, fix the electrical short in the basement, take me to church, find a job, mow the lawn, and don't forget your AA meetings".* Then pile on those internal challenges:

shame, guilt, depression, burnout, loneliness, paranoia, and frustration with your inability to cope with all the stress the sober world is lobbing at you. Is it any wonder that one begins to consider drinking and drugging a month after graduating from treatment? This is where recovery coaching is of great benefit.

Most people in recovery seldom make the connection between anger and substance use. Therefore they don't take the initiative to seek help for their anger issues. But what they don't realize is that their anger often is the underlying source of their addiction. drugs and alcohol fuels a chemical release in the body that can often mask anger. Once clients have stopped using substances, it can become easier for them to get more in touch with their anger issues constructively, something they previously couldn't address while dependent on substances.

Recovery coaches help clients see how anger plays into the addiction or relapse cycle process. Our job is to help clients identify anger stressors/triggers that often lead to relapse episodes and begin exploring techniques and alternatives for avoiding or managing potentially toxic situations. Recovery coaching is the best place to begin sorting out their feelings:

➤ Feelings of guilt over the pain they have caused friends and loved ones.

➤ Feelings of shame over what others might be thinking.

➤ Feelings of loneliness at being isolated, dropped out, and left out in the cold.

➤ Feelings of fear of a possible relapse.

➤

Anger Stressors/Triggers

Recovery coaching is hot on chalk-talks, role playing and homework assignments which clients can use to practice their new behaviors at home or in the workplace. We also call it "walking the talk". Recovery coaching is of the belief that if you want to change someone's behavior, you need to change yours first. It's about identifying your anger triggers and doing something constructive about them. Once done, the annoying factors that were bothering you before will begin to diminish.

One way to get clients to identify their anger stressors is to use the method of fact-checking their mistaken beliefs and attitudes regarding their current situation and the causes that may be preventing constructive communication. Solutions-based questioning is another good tool for fact-checking thinking errors. In this technique (as in all) the coach walks clients through a process of analyzing if the anger is real or imagined (a product of past conditioning) and if the anger is merely a cover-up for fear, shame or guilt. This is where one goes through a process of weighing the pros and cons or cost and benefits of displaying anger vs. just letting go. For some recovering people, anger left untreated can result in relapse.

A recovery coach helps clients:
> Identify mistaken attitudes (ABC model of Cognitive Restructuring).

> Investigate the nature of the anger that is preventing neutral or constructive communication (learned experiences).

> Learn the appropriate modes of expressing legitimate anger ("I" statements, fact-checking).

> Practice forgiveness and clean up any messes.

Things that upset us are called anger stressors or triggers. A stressor is like an electric shock that makes people react. Anger stressors are learned through past experiences taught by our parents, social settings, and negative experiences accumulated over time and which can become automatic. Those stressors are our first response to anger. But our first (automatic) response may not always be the best response, like hitting a candy machine because it took your dollar, only to experience a broken hand. Automatic stressors in one's life have a tendency to turn us into puppets. Every time someone or something pulls our string we react verbally or physically.

Anger-Provoking Phrases

- "You should…"
- "you shouldn't"
- "You're wrong…,"
- "I demand…,"
- "We can't…,"
- "We won't…,"
- "We never…,"

- Now, this is a no brainer."
- "You don't understand…,"
- "That's stupid…,"
- "What were you thinking…?"
- "You must be confused…,"
- "I'm too busy for this…," or
- "You have to…."

Anger Avoidance Pre-steps

✓ Identify any cognitive distortions in your own head.

✓ Recognize if you are really feeling angry or are your anger issues a cover-up for fear, shame or guilt.

✓ Analyze the costs and benefits of being angry vs. letting it go.

✓ Express feelings in a safe environment.

✓ Practice using "I" statements: "I get really angry when you…"

✓ Express your anger in person (tweeting, email, texting, or skyping do not count).

✓ Listen intently to the other person's side of the story.

✓ Practice a quick form of gaining control before meeting with the offender such as counting to 10, taking a walk or deep breathing.

Solutions-focused Questions coaches use in Anger Management

➢ "How did _____ make you feel?"

- ➤ "What goes on inside you when you think of confronting your ___? (a feeling, emotion, physical sensation, a memory.)"

- ➤ "Why do those feelings make you angry?"

- ➤ "Name three things that trigger your anger."

- ➤ "Name three things you could do to change the situation."

- ➤ "What's your worst case scenario here?"

- ➤ "What do you think is driving your angry responses?"

- ➤ "What learned-beliefs are behind your responses? How are those beliefs working for you?"

- ➤ "What is that critical voice inside you saying about this situation?"

- ➤ "List three things that could help you apply a neutral or positive response when anger stressors pops up."

Solutions-focused questioning about external barriers

- ➤ "What would be a better way to respond to _____?"

- ➤ "Name two things that are stopping you from_____? and what does that tell you?"

- ➤ "Name three things you need to reach your goal?"

- ➤ "When you got angry when you tried to make changes like this in the past, what got in the way? What does that tell you?"

Solutions-focused questioning about internal barriers

- ➤ "How did that make you feel?"

- ➤ "What goes on inside you when you think of confronting your feelings?

- ➤ "Why do those feelings make you angry?"

- ➤ "Name three things you could do to change the situation."

- "What's your worst case scenario here?"

- "What do you think is driving your angry responses?"

- "List three things that could help you apply a neutral or positive response to the next time an anger stressor pops up?"

H.A.L.T.: A Self-Care Tool

The first rule of recovery is that you must change your life. I first came across the acronym H.A.L.T. when I was working as a counselor in a chemical dependency treatment center in Los Angeles. H.A.L.T. stands for *H*ungry, *A*ngry, *L*onely, and *T*ired. Each one of these four physical or emotional conditions, if not taken care of, leaves an individual vulnerable for relapsing. I have found H.A.L.T. helpful in teaching clients each of the physical or emotional conditions that must be addressed in maintaining a safe recovery journey. Below is a detailed description of each condition in order for you to get the most out of this self-care tool.

Hunger describes the most obvious physical condition: a lack of food. But hunger can also point toward emotional needs: hunger for attention, comfort, understanding, or companionship. It is very important that we have others in our lives that can give us loving care.

Anger is a little bit more complex and the solution perhaps a bit more challenging for some. Here is the good news: there is nothing wrong with the feeling of anger! But here is the bad news: most of us have never learned how to express anger constructively. The way we express anger often takes on hugely destructive forms. We either turn the anger against ourselves or against others. Get your anger out, but do in non-defensive ways. You're in recovery now, but not everyone is going to be your best friend. Few will care that you are doing something about living sober. Trust me on that one!

Loneliness refers to isolating oneself. Being alone is a sure path to relapse. Building a new life is not an easy thing. We often have to deal with the left over problems from our past and go through mood swings, depression, and self-loathing on our sober journey. Begin building your own sober community or join one. If you're into A.A., find a sponsor, join a support group or a club (biking, jogging, meditation). Reward yourself with something that turns off the self-defeating chatter in your head. Don't find yourself alone because sometimes you may not be your best company.

Tiredness. We all have a tendency to ignore being tired at times. But what few people know is that tiredness makes a person weak and a weak person more susceptible to feelings of exhaustion, depression, and prone to cravings until (you guessed it) relapse occurs.

Finally, you must know that however bad your situation might be or how you are feeling, there is NO excuse good enough for returning to drinking and drugging. I give thanks to the people in Alcoholics Anonymous, where I think this acronym H.A.L.T. initially originated and allowing me the privilege of using it here for the benefit of us all.

MODULE TEN
Laws and Ethics

This module will enable coaches to:

➢ **Explore the importance of establishing professional boundaries.**

➢ **Understand the difference between ethical and legal issues and the fine line that separates both.**

➢ **Define the term dual relationship, and its potential damages in a coaching relationship.**

Laws and Ethics: What's the Difference?

There is a big difference between the law and ethics. An action can be unethical, for example, but not illegal. However, most actions that are illegal are also unethical. Even if unethical actions may not be illegal, they can still get you into a lot of legal hot water.

Word travels fast among professionals and their clients, and those professionals believed or suspected of exercising poor judgment soon find themselves blacklisted or sued for malpractice, even though their actions may not have been illegal. For example, accepting a gift from a client is not illegal, but now the relationship has shifted from professional to personal. The door has now been opened to bending rules and making exceptions for that client, which can have serious consequences both ethically and professionally.

You must become educated in the laws and professional ethics that pertain to the profession. Most health and human services professional associations have published codes of ethics that are applicable in their state. Although most states have their own published codes of ethics, no one can teach you good judgment. Still, it becomes our duty to remain objective, confidential and professional in all of our dealings with clients. The primary focus should be on always assisting clients with their recovery-related needs and goals, and never our own.

The Role of Ethics in Recovery Coaching

Success without integrity is still failure. Ethics is a system of moral standards and how they affect human conduct and made up of moral principles that decide and govern what is considered to be appropriate conduct for an individual or group. Ethical dilemmas occur where there are gray areas between right or wrong. Taking a spouse along on a business trip is a good example. Who then pays for the room? Do you split the charges between you and the company? Do you write it all off as a business expense? The IRS allows it, but is it ethical?

To some people, there can be more than one right or wrong answer to a moral dilemma. Several religions disagree with homosexuality for example, but there are others who don't. Some coaches may find themselves having to help recovering clients resolve issues relating to issues such as same-sex relationships and marriage. How does a coach who disagrees with these realities guide clients through their chosen dilemmas? Give it some thought.

Ethical Coaching Guidelines

A coach does not fix problems, but empowers clients to do so themselves partly through understanding and maintaining proper boundaries. The relationship between a recovery coach and a client is one of teacher-learner or giver-receiver of services and, if you notice carefully, the terms are always separated by a dash, meaning that lines are not to be crossed.

You may find that when clients come to a coaching session, they are often emotionally fragile, confused, vulnerable, lost or alone. Many are often stuck in a negative psychic place or are encountering mental barriers that are getting in the way of maintaining their sobriety. This can sometimes result in a client's misinterpretation of signals being sent by the coach. The coach may be the only person in a client's life who has truly listened, and this display of care can cause some clients to think a coach might want to take the relationship a bit further. This misinterpretation of signals is very common in all areas of behavioral science. Watch your signals and what you're putting out there.

Because coaches are human, they too can be caught in the trap of reading a client's signals the wrong way, but what every coach needs to understand is that as professionals, a signal misunderstood is never the client's fault. It is always presumed that the recovery coach knows right from wrong and must take all responsibility for maintaining a professional relationship with clients.

Ethical tips

- ✓ Social contact is to be limited to professional behavior. Always meet in an appropriate setting.
- ✓ Sexual or other intimate relationships is always prohibited. Period.
- ✓ Never take sides on moral or ethical issues.
- ✓ Do not bring your personal or professional issues into the coaching relationship.
- ✓ Minimal self-disclosure is always the best practice.
- ✓ Afford clients the dignity of risk and their right to fail.
- ✓ Assist clients in their efforts to grow beyond their current situation.
- ✓ Money or gifts are never to be exchanged or accepted.
- ✓ Do not do for clients what clients can do for themselves.
- ✓ Respect the rights of clients to use self-determination and to make decisions that they consider to be in their own best interest.
- ✓ Relate to all clients with empathy and understanding.
- ✓ Speak the truth (you'll have less to remember).
- ✓ Be worthy of trust, confidence and work consistently within the boundaries of a known and moral universe.
- ✓ Always nurture and support a relationship of equals.

(Source: NAADAC Code of Ethics; American Health Counselor's Association; Sober Network.)

Issues Relating to E-coaching and Teleconferencing

E-Coaching is a process involving any type of electronic communication as an alternative to face-to-face meetings. There are pros and cons to this type of communication. Most insurance companies (which are still mired in the 20th century) do not consider E-counseling, E-therapy, E-coaching or E-anything as an approved form of helping clients. Skype however, is rapidly being considered as an approved method of communicating with clients. Skype and in-person communication allows the coach to pick upon subtle cues such as body language, tone, and makes it easier to get an understanding of a clients' meaning behind the words.

About E-mail

E-mail and text messaging are rapidly becoming tools between coaching sessions. Most everyone carries a handheld communications device of some sort and all devices have email and text capabilities. It's portable and quick to use. In today's world, land lines are practically obsolete. If a client has a problem or is fearing a relapse, both of you can quickly engage in a brief conversation where you can offer support, and provide guidance within seconds. It's a great tool for communications to happen ASAP (stressing over a possible relapse on Friday night, emergency shelter, etc). Email is not a tool for back-and-forth coaching. Good, bad or indifferent, E-coaching is rapidly becoming acceptable as another important tool used to reach out to people in recovery who might otherwise never receive help.

INTERNATIONAL COACH FEDERATION: CODE OF ETHICAL STANDARDS

The International Coach Federation (ICF) has taken the lead in developing a definition and philosophy of coaching, as well as in establishing ethical standards among its members. Since many organizations are in the process of developing their own standards, Recovery Coach Academy as a proud member of ICF, RECOVERY COACH MASTERY recommends the use of the following ethical guidelines to all it's certified recovery coaches. *(membership information: www.coachfederation.org)*

Preamble

ICF Professional Coaches aspire to conduct themselves in a manner that reflects positively upon the coaching profession; are respectful of different approaches to coaching; and recognize that they are also bound by applicable laws and regulations.

Section 1: Professional Conduct At Large
As a coach:

1) I will not knowingly make any public statement that is untrue or misleading about what I offer as a coach or make false claims in any written documents relating to the coaching profession or my credentials or the ICF.

2) I will accurately identify my coaching qualifications, expertise, experience, certifications and ICF Credentials.

3) I will recognize and honor the efforts and contributions of others and not misrepresent them as my own. I understand that violating this standard may leave me subject to legal remedy by a third party.

4) I will, at all times, strive to recognize personal issues that may impair, conflict or interfere with my coaching performance or my professional coaching relationships. Whenever the facts and circumstances necessitate, I will promptly seek professional assistance and determine the action to be taken, including whether it is appropriate to suspend or terminate my coaching relationship(s).

5) I will conduct myself in accordance with the ICF Code of Ethics in all coach training, coach mentoring and coach supervisory activities.

6) I will conduct and report research with competence, honesty and within recognized scientific standards and applicable subject guidelines. My research will be carried out with the necessary consent and approval of those involved and with an approach that will protect participants from any potential harm. All research efforts will be performed in a manner that complies with all the applicable laws of the country in which the research is conducted.

7) I will maintain, store, and dispose of any records created during my coaching business in a manner that promotes confidentiality, security and privacy, and complies with any applicable laws and agreements

8) I will use ICF Member contact information (email addresses, telephone numbers, etc.) only in the manner and to the extent authorized by the ICF.

Section 2: Conflicts of Interest
As a coach:

9) I will seek to avoid conflicts of interest and potential conflicts of interest and openly disclose any such conflicts. I will offer to remove myself when such a conflict arises.

10) I will disclose to my client and his or her sponsor all anticipated compensation from third parties that I may pay or receive for referrals of that client.

11) I will only barter for services, goods or other non-monetary remuneration when it will not impair the coaching relationship.

12) I will not knowingly take any personal, professional or monetary advantage or benefit of the coach-client relationship, except by a form of compensation as agreed in the agreement or contract.

Section 3: Professional Conduct with Clients
As a coach:

13) I will not knowingly mislead or make false claims about what my client or sponsor will receive from the coaching process or from me as the coach.

14) I will not give my prospective clients or sponsors information or advice I know or believe to be misleading or false.

15) I will have clear agreements or contracts with my clients and sponsor(s). I will honor all agreements or contracts made in the context of professional coaching relationships.

16) I will carefully explain and strive to ensure that, prior to or at the initial meeting, my coaching client and sponsor(s) understand the nature of coaching, the nature and limits of confidentiality, financial arrangements, and any other terms of the coaching agreement or contract.

17) I will be responsible for setting clear, appropriate, and culturally sensitive boundaries that govern any physical contact I may have with my clients or sponsors.

18) I will not become sexually intimate with any of my current clients or sponsors.

19) I will respect the client's right to terminate the coaching relationship at any point during the process, subject to the provisions of the agreement or contract. I will be alert to indications that the client is no longer benefiting from our coaching relationship.

20) I will encourage the client or sponsor to make a change if I believe the client or sponsor would be better served by another coach or by another resource.

21) I will suggest my client seek the services of other professionals when deemed necessary or appropriate.

Section 4: Confidentiality/Privacy
As a coach:

22) I will maintain the strictest levels of confidentiality with all client and sponsor information. I will have a clear agreement or contract before releasing information to another person, unless required by law.

23) I will have a clear agreement upon how coaching information will be exchanged among coach, client and sponsor.

24) When acting as a trainer of student coaches, I will clarify confidentiality policies with the students.

25) I will have associated coaches and other persons whom I manage in service of my clients and their sponsors in a paid or volunteer capacity make clear agreements or contracts to adhere to the ICF Code of Ethics Part 2, Section 4: Confidentiality/Privacy standards and the entire ICF Code of Ethics to the extent applicable.

Part Three: The ICF Pledge of Ethics

As an ICF Professional Coach, I acknowledge and agree to honor my ethical and legal obligations to my coaching clients and sponsors, colleagues, and to the public at large. I pledge to comply with the ICF Code of Ethics and to practice these standards with those whom I coach.

If I breach this Pledge of Ethics or any part of the ICF Code of Ethics, I agree that the ICF in its sole discretion may hold me accountable for so doing. I further agree that my accountability to the ICF for any breach may include sanctions, such as loss of my ICF Membership and/or my ICF Credentials.

Approved by the Ethics and Standards Committee on October 30, 2008.
Approved by the ICF Board of Directors on December 18, 2008.

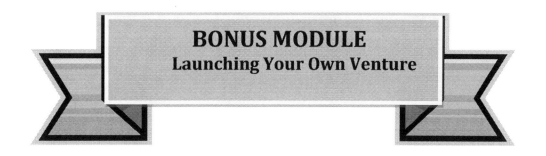

BONUS MODULE
Launching Your Own Venture

This module will enable coaches to:

➢ Explore basics of launching a Recovery Coaching career.

➢ Understand the importance of marketing.

➢ Examine the use 30 effective marketing tools.

➢ Implement successful strategies for attracting clients.

➢ Prepare an elevator speech.

LAUNCHING A COACHING CAREER

Welcome to the world of recovery coaching. Did you know that in our lifetime we typically change careers ten times? So it come as no surprise that many people have been considering making a shift from their current profession to one they can enjoy and share their special gift: a passion for helping and empowering others. Through recovery coaching you will be able to do just that, while at the same time learning more about yourself. You've done that through this training program already. But a Professional Recovery Coaching Certificate is not enough to attract clients. The key to being a successful recovery coach is to combine your powerful coaching skills with proven business strategies, primarily marketing. Theory and personae are only one half of the equation. Let me just say that people who attempt to start a coaching business on their own are in for a hard grind.

Don't follow your passion...live it!

Because recovery coaching is a combination of art and technology, it may require that you utilize the services of a mentor. Let me also add that the most successful professional coaches treat their coaching as a professional passion, not a calling. You will charge a fee for your service and your clients will expect results out of the business relationship. So it will serve you well to learn what you need and master it completely.

Plan to spend between $3000-$5000 per year in your own coach training and mentoring. As a new coach, you will encounter situations that may shock, stump or throw you for a loop. A mentor has *been-there-done-that* and can assist you in handling special situations effectively and professionally.

Rules to Live By

Nolan Bushnell, the founder of Chuck E. Cheese was attributed to saying, *"An entrepreneur tends to bite off a little more than he can chew hoping he'll quickly learn how to chew it."* This could not be truer than the coaching business. Don't start a coaching practice unless you're going to be passionate about it. If you have an exit strategy as a backup, then it's not your passion and you shouldn't do it.

You must lay out a plan that shows you how your practice will become financially feasible and in what time span. Don't be too quick about rushing out and renting an office. Recovery coaches often work out of their home office, they meet at Starbucks or the library and communicate through Skype, phone or e-mail. You are not building and empire. You are merely starting a business.

How Hard Are You Willing to Work?

That is an important question to ask yourself. I could sit here and tell you that starting your own recovery (or any niche) business will be easy and that you're going to make a lot of money in ninety days or less, but I won't. I'd be cautious of anyone who would promise you that. There are programs on the internet that promise you it will be easy. If you find one, hit your delete key because like any other career passion, it won't be.

Remember that overnight success takes about ten years of hard labor. Your journey will be difficult and you will have to make some sacrifices. Once you have been confirmed as a Recovery Coach and awarded your coaching certification, you may find yourself having to conduct your coaching business on the side; at Starbucks or the library, after work until you become established. That's how most coaches get started. What makes this all very interesting is how the principles you will be learning as you launch your new business are the same principles you will be teaching your clients as they struggle in the pursuit of their dreams: *obstacles, personal and external barriers, and those times you thought of giving up.* It's going to take determination and intentionality. It's going require hanging out in government centers, with a backpack filled with advertising flyers, buying a lot of coffee to the *gatekeepers* who have access judges, public defenders, probation officers. Then there are the naysayers the treatment elite who claim they already do what you do and who may be looking at you as a threat to their business: *"Coaching, what's that?"*

Eight Principles for Business Success:

1. **Nurture your vision.** A vision keeps you focused.
2. **Work harder than others.** The harder you work the harder it is to give up.
3. **Be committed 24-7.** You must have a well-defined purpose...a driving hunger. Do not become sidetracked by *this-is-the-way-we've-always-done-it* thinkers. Listen to conventional wisdom, but then walk away. Sleep on it and then decide with clarity, instinct and purpose.
4. **Be reliable** and always stay true to your word. Your clients will trust you. Meet all of your business, social and moral obligations punctually, honestly and honorably.
5. **Persevere.** Maintain a never-give-up attitude. Be tough on yourself. Demand the best and highest standards of yourself (and others).
6. **Be inspirational** to others. Give and you shall receive. It will all come back to you four-fold. You were put on this earth for a purpose. Don't get so high on yourself and your successes.
7. **Risk a little.** What you risk shows what you value
8. **Be human**. Remember to experience the journey as well as the results. Goals are important, but don't miss out on all the great experiences going on around you right now, because when you finally arrive to your destination, you'll realize that some of the greatest lessons learned, some of the great people you've, and the values you have gained were found in the journey getting there.

FROM PAPER TO PLAN

This is the point where you may have to return to your own empowerment vision statements section and rewrite what your business niche will look like in the next ten years. Begin to clearly define your business idea. State its purpose and goal(s) using clear and simple language. Examine your motives. Why are you doing this at this stage of your life? Are you willing to commit an inordinate amount of hours, discipline, and frustration that are common in owning a business? If so, let's begin.

Market Research

Market research does not have to be complicated or expensive, but it has to be done. Check out other agencies, entrepreneurs in the coaching field to determine whether there is an adequate number of potential clients in need of your coaching niche and can it support a recovery coaching business. Find out your competition: clinics, treatment facilities, A.A., outpatient and/or counseling centers. Just know that you are *the new kid in town* and as such, may receive resistance from the competition. Your competition can be very territorial, and traditional in their delivery: *"This is the way we've always done it and we don't need any new, untested programs competing with us."*

Create a Business Plan

Business Plan? Oh no! Many budding entrepreneurs are business plan phobic. Please don't panic. A well-written business plan can get you a long way in setting up shop in your community and produce clients soon after you open your door. There are several non-profits that can guide you in the preparation of a business plan for a small fee (or free). An organization you can to use is called SCORE at www.score.org. And there are others you can access online.

A business plan for a recovery coaching business should not exceed twelve pages and, at minimum, should include the following nine items:

1. Executive summary: a one or two page overview of your business and its activities. Include your goal followed by two or three key objectives.
2. Business description: The condition of substance abuse and demographics in the community you will be serving and how you see your business growing in the next 5-10 years.
3. Product or Service: Describe the core nature of your service/business.
4. Competition: Honesty describes your competition and how/why your business will differ from other providers.
5. Marketing Strategies: This is the longest section and describes how you will access the marketplace: tradeshows, media marketing, a website, etc.
6. Management and Personnel: This explains your staffing formula and how you will manage your business. Remember that not every coach is a good businessman and not every businessman can be a good coach, but rarely can anyone be both. Someone has to be the bean-counter.
7. Financial Data: This pertains to a balance sheet.
8. Investment considerations: How much capital have you put up? Who are the investors? How much will investors receive in return?
9. Testimonials: Testimonials from prior/current clients, charts, newspaper clips and media reports which are relevant to your business can be added.

Writing your own business plan-Exercise

Write a brief business descriptor about your business:

Executive Summary:

Business description:

Business structure: (Non-profit; LLC; Full partnership...see next page)

Specific service provided:

Identify the competition and the competitive edge you have over others:

Marketing Strategies:

Management/Personnel:

Financial start-up data:

Name other investors:

Testimonials from supporters:

(use more paper if necessary)

Choosing a Business Structure

- ➤ Sole Proprietorship: The owner and the business are one in the same.
- ➤ Partnership: A business with more than one owner; divides losses and profits equally among partners.
- ➤ Incorporation: A safer way of doing business and is a state-charter owned by shareholders.
    - o Advantages: Personal assets are protected.
    - o Disadvantages: Profits can be subject to double taxation (once on the corporation, and again when the individual share holders are paid.)
    - o Best of all options: Limited Liability Corp. (LLC). No ownership restrictions; no double taxation; easier access to capital as opposed to partnership; less formal and less paperwork.

*"Success is about finding a livelihood
that brings you joy, self-sufficiency
and a sense of contributing to the world."*

The Importance of Marketing Skills

There is a world of difference between knowing how to coach and knowing how to market your services. Even if you believe you are the greatest coach on the planet, if you don't have a good marketing strategy, your business will have the lifespan of a banana on a shelf. Also, giving away free coaching seminars are for amateurs. Other professionals don't give away their services, why should you? Most professionals do, however give courtesy consultations to help clients decide whether to contract with them or not, but that's different and coaches can do the same.

The coaches who have been most successful in their field have either good marketing skills in their background or know where to hire those services. It's understandable that most coaches fear being viewed as used car dealers when marketing their services, but truth be told, nothing happens in our business until someone agrees to do business with you.

Eight Generic Marketing Questions

1. *What are two challenges you are currently facing?*
2. *How do you think you would benefit from partnering mentoring with a recovery coach?*
3. *Would you like to know what a recovery coach does?*
4. *Is there something I could help you with today?*
5. *Would having some support with your problem be helpful?*
6. *What are some strategies you have thought of to help you with your current challenge?*
7. *Would it help you to talk to a coach about that, or..."*

FILL YOUR STADIUM

Your coaching will only be as good as you are. Remember the five life domains in our Whole Life Recovery module? Be those! Always strive to nurture and keep in balance your physical, mental, emotional, social, and spiritual domains. That is one way to attract clients that are ready to partake of what you have to offer. The way you carry yourself and your positive attitude is what will inspire others to want to learn more about what you do. Do you need a list of credentials to be a great coach? Not necessarily. Clients who have made a successful recovery are sufficient enough credentials. Just learn and apply the skills you have been taught and deliver 110% of what you promise and your client-base will take care of itself. Clients want you to be a straight-shooter, caring, and relentless in your efforts to help them change.

How to Fill the Seats in Your Stadium

1. Obtain appropriate training and certification.
2. Host a Lunch-N-Learn and invite professionals in the helping professions.
   a. Ask them for 3 referrals each.
   b. Collect their business cards and add them to your email list.
3. Lead a workshop for your friends, clients, and prospects.
4. Create a strong web presence.
5. Create a dynamite newsletter.
6. Speak on radio talk shows.
7. Speak on those local early Sunday morning shows.
8. Write an editorial for your local newspaper.
9. Send out press releases. Create a press kit.
10. Learn and use recovery coaching language.
11. Network with other coaches.
12. Set up an advisory group.
13. Speak to prospects in terms of benefits not features of your business.
14. Be straightforward and honest.
15. Budget 10% of your budget for advertising.

16. Link your site to Internet search engines.
17. Link your site to other coaches and them to you.
18. Offer to teach a unit for other coaches.
19. Write a book, handbook, parent booklet.
20. Write a magazine article or article in local, neighborhood newspaper.
21. Offer free tele-classes
22. Offer free CD's.
23. Utilize YouTube.
24. Host a virtual community.
25. Know what you're selling.
26. Offer Skype coaching.
27. Establish a *Virtual University;* a software product used for teleconferencing/training from your home or office
28. Arrange for a credit card merchant account right off your Ipad.
29. Offer trainer-of-trainer options.
30. Scholarship a client or two in your training as good will .

Website Marketing

A website should do the talking for your coaching enterprise.
Five things your website can begin doing:

1. Capture the visitors email.
2. Permit visitors to sign up for free material.
3. Help the visitor buy your product(s) online.
4. Design a FAQ section.
5. Offer a free E-newsletter.

(Sources: Coachville.com; The Coaching Starter Kit, 2013)

Clients Are Looking for You

The topic title is correct. Clients are looking for someone they can trust to help them make the proper changes in their lives. One of life's truisms is: *with the perfect amount of support, a person can do just about anything.* That is the first steps in helping potential clients know you are the person for the task of helping them fulfill their dreams. The challenge for many coaches is that many are not trained in marketing their services. It doesn't matter if you're the greatest coach on the planet, if you don't have decent marketing skills you're coaching career is going to have a short lifespan. Selling skills will help your perspective clients make a decision about you being the professional they have been seeking. Below are a few marketing tips that can help.

Top Five Objections Raised by Potential Clients

1. *"I don't have time to work with a coach."*
   Possible responses: *"I'd like to help you with that. What does your daily schedule look like?"* Or: *"How healthy is the stress in your current schedule? What is draining your energy the most?"*

2. *"I can't afford any coaching fees."*

   Possible response: *"How much do you think would be affordable for you to get started?"*

3. *"I don't know what I would work on. I've already been to therapy and that was no help."*
   Possible responses: *"I'm sorry to hear that. What has been causing you your greatest concern? What if you could spend one hour with someone who could...?"* Or: *"What are the three biggest recovery challenges you are currently facing?"*

4. "I'm not sure a coach can help me."
   Possible responses: *"Really, why?"* Or: *"Which part do you think a coach could help you with?"*

5. *"I already have a (mentor, sponsor, sober buddy).*
   Possible responses: *Wonderful! What sorts of things are you focusing on? Or:*
   "What is it that you aren't working on with him/her that would still need some strategic support?"

Top Five Questions to Ask a Prospective Client

The key to drawing people to you is in the *positioning and structuring of the interview and closure*:

> Positioning: *"First of all, I'm not selling anything. I am a wellness and recovery coach. My job is to help people reach their greatest potential through sobriety."*

> Structuring: Pertains to the ability to help potential clients determine if you are a good fit. A good way to get them to buy in is to ask consultative questions:

1. *"Assuming you have enough financial and emotional support to__, what is the biggest change you would like to make in your life?"*
2. *"How do you define success for yourself?*
3. *"How is the way you are solving your problem(s) working for you?"*
4. *"What are the three biggest challenges you are currently facing?"*

Closure: pertains to getting the potential client to commit.

1. *"How ready are you to begin tackling those challenges?"*
2. *"What will it take to get you to the next step?"*
3. *Would you be willing to meet over coffee or my office to explore a few options that could help with....?"(present your business card)*

Elevator Speeches

Elevator speeches are short one or two minute presentations recovery coaches use to describe what we do and to generate interest with curious strangers. At a social gathering, someone asks, *"What do you do?"* That's an elevator speech opportunity. Elevator speeches will be critical to your success as a coach, so you must have several of them rehearsed and ready at all times. The worse thing a coach can do is to stumble through an elevator speech unprepared when an opportunity suddenly presents itself.

Elevator speeches won't happen without advance mental rehearsal. For every key point you wish to touch on, identify one or two salient points and them rehearse them. Assign each point a little mental nametag so you can retrieve it later. That's it! You just created the skeleton of your elevator speech.

Don't miss out on an opportunity to showcase what you do. Below are thirty second responses used with clients, reporters, and inquiring minds:

✓ *"Thanks for asking. I am a wellness and recovery coach. I help people in recovery rise above their compulsive or addictive disorders.*

✓ *I am not a therapist. I offer guidance, hope, and support to clients experiencing transitions in life or needing help meeting their life goals.*

✓ *We (I) help clients reach the goals that they have outlined for themselves.*

✓ *We (I) maintain a collaborative relationship with our clients and believe that an ongoing, supportive relationship works best for our clients.*

✓ *We (I) offer 4-5 sessions per month be it in-person, email, or using Skype technology.*

✓ *We (I) share with our community by serving as a resource for clients and we do best when we can put our clients in touch with other professionals in the community.*

Key elements of an elevator speech or press conference

Elevator speeches need to answer your listeners' unspoken question, *"Why should I listen to this?"* Before responding to an inquiry, be clear on your topic:

✓ Don't dilute the power of your response with extraneous information.

✓ Be brief, concise and use compelling language. Your listener is not looking to fill a bucket full of what you know or who you are. A mere tea cup should be sufficient.

✓ Make it memorable. One simple way to make your elevator speech memorable is to use numbers: "There are two or three key elements of what I do as a coach..."

✓ Teach them something new about what you do. Whet their appetite by citing statistics. Engage them by offering your card and end with: *"Look us up on our web page. We offer a free newsletter and a half-hour free consultation."*

CHALK TALK

Writing the Elevator Speech-Exercise

With your coaching partner, practice using five examples of an elevator speech pertaining to your area of coaching expertise:

1._____

_____

2._____

_____

3._____

_____

4._____

_____

5._____

_____

You Don't Have to Accept Every Client

Before accepting a client, you must first determine if the client is the best fit for you. We aren't all experts at determining who benefits most from our coaching services. However there are some quality indicators based on instinct, feelings, and verbal/nonverbal cues that surface during an introductory conversation. Here are a few examples:

✓ Is this person still using?

✓ Does this person appear to be a danger to himself or others?

✓ Is this person ready for a coach or in need of someone more specialized?

✓ What are the three things I know I can do to help the client?

✓ Is this person likely to stick around for the first ninety days? (Six months?)

✓ Will this person's participation *enhance* my practice and reputation?

✓ Using your best judgment, is this person capable of making the monthly fee payments on time? Again, flake-factors to be considered.

If your ship is too slow getting here, swim out to meet it.

-APPENDIX-

-SAMPLE COACHING AGREEMENT-

Coaching Agreement:
This agreement is made between Coach's Name ("Coach"), and Client's Name ("Client"). Both parties agree to the following:

Commitment:
What is Recovery Coaching?
Recovery Coaching is an ongoing alliance between a Coach and a Client. The opportunity for success for the coaching Client dramatically increases because changing habits and perspectives creates far reaching possibilities. Coaching is a process that is established and reinforced throughout the coaching relationship. Coaching is a structure that facilitates the process and fulfillment in the areas of personal, professional and/or spiritual development, as determined by the Client. The Client and Coach agree that the coaching relationship will be designed together.
Coaching is for individuals who are emotionally and psychologically healthy and who want to break down personal barriers, make changes and move forward. Coaching is not advice, therapy or counseling, or about rescue. Coaching is about growth and changing your life's direction.
By entering this relationship, the Coach and Client acknowledge that the Client wants to make significant progress and change in his/her life. Because progress and change happen at rates that are unique to each individual, the Coach and client commit to working with each other for an initial three-month period although additional sessions are encouraged. This allows the coaching relationship necessary time to develop and progress through objectives, plateaus, obstacles and successes that occur.
As your wellness and recovery coach, I agree to maintain a professional, and collaborative relationship within the parameters of our coaching alliance and together, work on whatever is preventing you from meeting your goal(s). I will be your fact-checker and accountability partner. Our relationship will be based on trust, communication, and concrete action.
This is What I am Prepared to do for You:
1. One 30 minute orientation session at no-cost to you, the client to determine if we are a good fit for each other.
2. One weekly in-person (if local) or Skype wellness/life/recovery coaching session (typically 60 minutes).
3. Development of a personalized action or recovery plan (if needed).
4. One Friday or Saturday afternoon weekend planning phone call for sober-living, typically 15-20 minutes. (Weekends are the most relapse-prone days of the week.)
5. One partner/family meeting per month as part of your sessions, if desired.

Fee for Service:

In order to gain the most from our collaborative coaching relationship, we have agreed that you commit to coaching Write down agreed upon duration of sessions. The agreed upon fee is whatever your fee is per week, which includes all services listed above. Agreements:

- ✓ Your Company will provide the coaching sessions through Your Title, ex.recovery/life/wellness coach/ Name.
- ✓ Your Company will provide coaching that is a professional client-coach relationship   designed to facilitate the creation and development of personal, professional or business goals and to develop and carry out a strategy/plan for moving towards those goals.
- ✓ E-mails are welcome between sessions if you would like to share a success, have urgent questions or an issue.
- ✓ You agree to pay the Fees as set out in this Agreement.
- ✓ You agree to call or meet the Coach at the specified times.
- ✓ You agree to be honest and open, to believe in yourself and to adopt a more enthusiastic and positive outlook on life from this moment onwards.
- ✓ You are truly committed to change and agree to take responsibility for your life, choices and actions.
- ✓ You enter into this Agreement with the full understanding that you are solely responsible for creating your own results. You understand that failure to meet your goals (in whole or part) cannot be guaranteed and no warranties are given or implied.
- ✓ You are aware that coaching is not counseling, psychotherapy, psychoanalysis or any other form of mental health care treatment or therapy, nor is it to be used as a substitute for professional advice by legal, medical, financial, business or other qualified professionals.
- ✓ If appropriate, you will seek independent professional guidance in the areas indicated above and understand that all decisions and actions in these areas are your sole responsibility.
- ✓ Each coaching session agenda belongs to you. If any session is not heading in the direction you would like, or if you have a concern with the way the sessions are proceeding, you have the right to let the Coach know immediately.

Ethics and Confidentiality

1.   Any notes the Coach makes during the Session or about you are kept confidential.
2.   The Coach will not use or disclose the information you share with them during Your   Sessions, except as authorized by You or as required by law.
3.   You understand that on occasion Your Company's Name may receive anonymous generalized information for training or consultation purposes with other Coaching professionals. Your identity and any information about you will remain entirely confidential.

Administrative agreement:

1.   The session may be refused if payment has not been made as required by this Agreement.

2.   If it is necessary for either you or the Coach to reschedule a session this will be done by phone at least 48 hours before the scheduled session.
3.   You will be charged for missed sessions which are not rescheduled in accordance with this agreement, except in exceptional circumstances (at the Coach's discretion).
4.   If you are late for a Session, the Session will complete at the scheduled time. Termination:
   a)   You or Your Company's Name may cancel this Agreement in writing (by email or letter), giving at least 7 clear days notice. In the event that you owe money to Your Name at the time of cancellation, full payment will be due at the time of cancellation.
   b)   In the unlikely event that this Agreement is cancelled before all the Sessions have been completed, you will be refunded only for the sessions you have not yet attended at the rate of 50%, (or whatever you have agreed upon) of the agreed rate.
   c)   Upon termination of this Agreement Your Company shall immediately cease to be liable to you in respect of the coaching Sessions.

General:
In the event of you choosing to feel mental, physical or emotional distress (or related ailment or condition) which you believe to be related either directly or indirectly to the coaching sessions, you will not hold Your Company liable for any loss or cost incurred by you (or any person related to you). You will indemnify Your Company in the event of any such claim, (except as expressly set out in this Agreement Your Company) will have no liability to you. This Agreement reflects the entire agreement and understanding between you and Your Company regarding the matters in this Agreement.

Your Intent to Change Your Situation:
1.   You will make every effort to ensure you are at your peak mental, physical and emotional state for each session.
2.   You will attend with a willingness to work and try new ways of learning.
3.   You are willing to explore, challenge and change thoughts, feelings and actions that you recognize as self-defeating.
4.   You understand your coach will be focused on you and your best interests as a whole, not just your goals.
5.   You are willing to give the coach the benefit of the doubt and wholeheartedly try new concepts or different ways of doing/approaching things.
6.   You recognize the value of any investment you make in your personal development.

I understand the above:

      Client signature_____

RELAPSE PREVENTION PLANNING

Relapse does not have to be an expensive revolving door! Preventing relapse requires an awareness of our inner struggles, especially with denial. Clients in recovery are taught that they are the only persons that can keep themselves clean. Clients are also brought to an awareness that one doesn't recover from an addiction by stopping using. One recovers by creating a new life where it is easier to not use. If they do not begin to explore new ways of creating a new life, then all the factors that brought them to their addiction will eventually catch up with them again.

Seven Stages of Relapse

Relapse is a process NOT an event. Relapse begins in your head and usually starts days, weeks or months in advance.

Seven Categories for Relapse

1. False Recovery or insufficient effort. This category includes episodic users/drinkers and others who modify their use patterns to avoid consequences, but never make a 100% commitment to recovery.

2. Too many problems, not enough resources or programs. Many arrive in treatment sincere, but are overwhelmed by their reality.

3. Sobriety skill deficiencies. Not serious enough to want to learn how to be sober: avoiding people, places, situations, basic living skills keeping appointments, anger management, support system development, and advanced living skills such as developing new friendships, and career development.

4. Sobriety belief deficiencies. Stopped putting what was learned into continued practice (maintenance) or belief that relapsing is just a matter of when and does not give 100% effort to abstinence.

5. Priority conflict. Life gets better, one feels better and has not been tempted to use in years, so you move on without keeping grounded with your recovery support.

6. Persistent problems or difficult life. Prior abuse as a child and continued abuse issues as an adult or an untreated depression or coexisting mental issues are all good examples. Sometimes it isn't easy to determine in aftercare.

7. Sudden life changes. A sudden turning point enters a recovering person's life. It can often start with a positive change (new job, new baby) or it could start with a negative life change (divorce, death in family, suddenly unemployed, or a forced relocation) which is followed by a change in daily patterns, a change in one's support system, and the development of situational depression.

(Adapted from: Steve Casey, MSEd,LADC,LISW. 2009; *Last Relapse. Missing Pieces Workbook;* Earnie Larsen: *Now That You're Sober, 2009.* Terence T. Gorski: *Starting Recovery with Relapse Prevention, 2012.*)

Identifying Relapse Warning Signs

You don't have to change everything in your life. But there are a few people, things and behaviors that have been getting you into trouble, and they will continue to get you into trouble until you let them go. The more you try to hold onto your old life in recovery, the less well you will do.

This worksheet is designed to help you identify any relapse warning signs that you may have while in recovery...and life. Please answer all these questions with honesty and as open as you can. Denial can always keep you from being honest with yourself.

1. Who are the people that you are most likely to drink or drug with?
2. Who are the people most difficult to separate from?
3. Who in your life is associated with your addiction?
4. Name three (3) ways you could communicate with these people the fact that you are in recovery and are committed to staying sober and that they need to respect that.
5. Name five internal feelings place you at great risk of drinking or drugging?
6. Name five external (social/relationship) situations or events place you at risk for a relapse?
7. How do you spend your time when you're bummed out or having the urge to use?
8. How have your behaviors changed in the last few days (weeks/months)?
9. Name five differences in thoughts and attitudes in the last few days (weeks/months).
10. Name five possible consequences if you were to relapse today?

There are going to be times when you will have the urges to use. Tell someone. Call a friend, a support, or someone in recovery. Share with them what you're going through. The great thing about sharing is that the minute you start to talk about what you're thinking and feeling, your urges begin to disappear. They don't seem quite as big and you don't feel as alone.

Take ten minutes to think of how you can begin formulating an action plan. Using the following template, begin to formulate your plan and share it with your coach, sponsor, group, a recovering partner, therapist or your significant other(s). Relapse ends here…with you!

Relapse Prevention in One's First Year of Recovery

A list of important goals for your first year of recovery. Use it as a reminder and to help you stay on track in the days and months ahead. Remember that recovery is about progress not perfection.

- Accept that you have an addiction.
- Avoid high-risk situations.
- Practice honesty in your life.
- Learn to avoid high-risk situations.
- Learn to ask for help.
- There are many paths to recovery. The most difficult doing it alone.
- Practice calling friends before you have cravings.
- Become actively involved in self-help recovery groups.
- Replace using friends.
- Make time for you and your recovery.
- Celebrate your small victories.
- Develop healthy eating and sleeping habits.
- Discover how to have fun clean and sober.
- Make new recovery friends and bring them into your life.
- Deal with cravings by "playing the tape forward" What will happen if you start?
- Find ways to distract yourself when you have cravings.
- Physical activity helps many aspects of recovery.
- Develop strategies for social environments where drinking is involved.
- Develop tolerance and compassion for others and for yourself.
- Begin to give back and help others once you have a solid recovery.

(Steve Melemis, *I Want to Change My Life*, 2012. Terence Gorski, *Cognitive Restructuring for Addiction Workbook, 2004. G. Alan, Relapse Prevention: Theoretical Rational…1982*)

RELAPSE PREVENTION

-Action Plan-

1. With a sheet a paper, draw a line down the middle and on the left side of the line make a list of ten (10) things that could trigger your addiction.

2. On the other side of the line write down possible solutions to each trigger. The solutions depend on what works for you.

3. Write down the names and phone numbers of at least five (5) people you know you can call if you have the urge to relapse.

4. Write down at least five (5) activities that could get your mind off your urges. Make sure the activities are things that are relaxing and that you really enjoy (music/exercise/yoga/etc)

5. List what you plan on doing in case you do relapse, such calling your recovery coach/sponsor/friend/relative. Calling someone you can rely upon can help control or change the situation.

6. Make copies of your action plan and share them with the names you have listed. Keep it your purse or wallet and accessible in case of an emergency. Being prepared for a relapse is the best way to prevent one!

Cut this out and stick in your purse/wallet or lock it into your Ipad or Iphone.

1. **Names, phone numbers or email addresses of 5 persons I can call in case of an urge to relapse:**

2. **Places you can go immediately to help extinguish any urges:**

-ENDORSEMENTS-

Many people describe our Recovery Coach Mastery training experience as a turning point in both their professional and personal lives. Recovery Coach Mastery may rank among the most comprehensive and effective training that you have ever experienced.

"This was a major turning point in both my personal and professional life."
(J. Buerkle, Social Worker, Canoga Park, Ca.)

"I have found new ways to help people to move forward in their recovery."
(H.A.J. Alcoholic Anonymous, Sponsor)

"Dr. Lou is the Indiana Jones of recovery coaching."
(Franklin Scott, District Attorney)

"Since I am a half world away I feel blessed to have learned extremely well-developed materials that were presented in such a practical, yet professional way. I can start using these tools immediately. Thank you Dr. Lou!"
(Leigh-Ann Brierley, Educator; Johannesburg, South Africa)

"Thank you for kick-starting my new career."
(M.G. Franklin, Chicago IL. Career Couch)

"Dr. Gonzales will continue to serve as a pioneer in the emerging and evolving world of recovery coaching. Thank you for allowing me to participate."

(F.L.W. Probation Officer, Manitoba Canada)

Dr. Gonzales' training seamlessly incorporated his 30 plus years experience with approachability and humor. He was able to introduce sophisticated concepts and theories in an engaging and effective style. (Shira Goldberg, B.S., RRW; California)

Dr. Gonzales provided me with the confidence and skills I needed to help me grow in my new profession. I now have the tools and insight to be even more valuable, both personally as well as professionally.

(Earsie, Cowart, counselor, Compton California)

Sources and References

Avants SK, Warburton LA, Margolin A. *Spiritual and religious support in recovery from addiction among HIV-positive injection drug users.* Journal of Psychoactive Drugs. 2001

Abraham Twerski. (1998) *Addictive Thinking: Understanding Self-Deception.*

Arredondo, P. (1996). *Multicultural Counseling Competencies as Tools to Address Oppression and Racism.*

Bannink Fredrike. (1999). *1001 Solution-focused Questions.*

Benjamin Chapman. (1994). *Characteristics of Effective Counselors and Therapists.*

Beck, Aaron. *Cognitive Behavior Therapy. Second edition. 1994.*

Beck, Aaron. (1999). *Prisoners of Hate.*

Beck, T.F., & Yager, G.G. (1982). *Three models of Confrontation Skills Training. (presentation) American Eduational Research Association.*

Berg J.S. (1996) *Cognitive Therapy: Basics and Beyond.*

Berg I.K. & Dolan y. (2001). *Working with the problem drinker.*

Berne, Eric. (1967). *Games People Play; I'm O.K., You're O.K.*

Cepeda, L.M. (1993). *Person-centered therapy: Practice and Training.*

Chapman, R.J. (1993). *Counseling the Drug Dependent Client.*

Cloud, W. & Granfield, R. (1994). *Natural recovery from addictions: Treatment implications.*

Cormier S. (2012) *Counseling Strategies strategies and interventions.*

Coyhis, D.L. (1993). *Recovery From the Heart. Hazelden.*

David Kiersey & Marilyn Bates. *Please Understand Me: Character and Temperament Types.*

DeMars, P.A. (1993). *An Occupational Life Skills Curriculum for Native Americans.*

D'Andrea, M., & Daniels, J. (1994). *The many faces of racism: A cognitive developmental framework.*

Ellis, Albert. *A Guide to Rational Living.*

Gendlin, Eugene. (2007) University of Chicago, The Focusing Institute.

Gonzales, L.D. (2012). *They Can't Be Loved Into Sobriety.*

Gordon, J.U. (1998). *Managing Multiculturalism in Substance Abuse Services.*

Gorski, Terence. *Straight Talk about Addiction.*

Gorski, Terence & Merlene Miller. (2001). *Staying Sober: A Guide for Relapse Prevention.*

Gingerich, W. J. & Eisengart, S, (2000). *Solution-Focused Brief Therapy: A Review of the Outcome Research.*

Guiliene Kraft, Ph.D. for the Caravel Institute (2006). *Cultural Considerations in Short-term Cognitive Behavioral Therapy.*

Thomas Harbin (2001) *Beyond Anger: A Guide for Men.*

Harrow, J. (1995) *Confrontation: The Dark Mirror.*

Koski-Jannes A, Turner N. *Factors influencing recovery from different addictions.* Addiction Research. 1999

Larsen, Earnie. *Now That you're Sober: Week by Week Guide From Your Recovery Coach.*

Leahy, Robert, PhD. *Cognitive Therapy Techniques: A Practitioners Guide*

Leaman,D. (1978). *Confrontation in Counseling: Personnel & Guidance Journal.*

Loveland, David. *Manual for Recovery Coaching and Personal Recovery Plan* 2005.

William Miller and Stephen Rollnick. (2002). *Motivational Interviewing: Preparing People for Change,* 2nd Edition .

Mann, Cathleen A. (2003). *Therapeutic groups versus 12-step groups: An analysis of the AA prototype.*

Miller, W. R., & Rollnick, S. (2009). *Ten Things That Motivational Interviewing is not.*

Miller, W.R., & Rollnick, S. (2013). *Helping People Change; 3rd Edition.*

NAMI. National Alliance on Mental Illness; 2004. *Evidence-practices and Multicultural Mental Health.*

Portia Nelson. *"There's a Hole in My Sidewalk: The Romance of Self-Discovery".*

White, W., Boyle, M. & Loveland, D. (2002). *Addiction as chronic disease: From rhetoric to clinical application.* Alcoholism Treatment Quarterly, 20(3/4), 107-130.

White, W. & Kurtz, E. (2005). *The varieties of recovery experience.*

Prochaska, J., Norcross, J., & DiClemente, C. (1995). *Changing for Good.* New York: HarperCollins Books.

Rapp, R.C., Siegal, H.A., & Fisher, J.H. (1992). *A strengths-based model of case management/advocacy: adpating a mental health model to practice work with persons who have substance abuse problems.*

Rosenberg, D.B., *Building Motivational Interviewing Skills: A Practitioner Workbook, 2012.*

Schuyler, Alida. 2012, *Making Recovery Work. Crossroads Coaching.*

Sciacca K.(1997). *Removing Barriers: Dual Diagnosis Treatment and Motivational Interviewing.*

Sobell, M. B., & Sobell, L. C. (1993). *Problem drinkers: guided self-change treatment.*

Stoltzfus, T.*(2008) Coaching Questions: A Coaches Guide to Powerful Asking Questions.*

Sue, D.W. & Sue, D. (2003). *Counseling the culturally different: Theory and practice.*

Thompson, M., Ellis, R., & Wildavsky,A. (1990). *Cultural theory.* San Francisco: Westview.

Walter, J.L. & Peller, J.E. (1992). *Becoming Solution-Focused in Brief Therapy.*

Wampold & Bhati (2004). *Attending to the Omissions. A Historical Examination of Evidence-Based Practice Movements.*

White, William. (1996). *Sponsor, Recovery Coach, and Addiction Counselor: The Importance of Role Clarity and Role Integrity.*

Young Mark. (2008). *Learning the Art of Helping (4th edition).*

Quotations attributed to: Rick Warren, Andy Rooney, Robin Williams, Albert Ellis, John F. Kennedy, Edward Abbey, Tony Robbins, Victor Hugo, Elizabeth Berg and others.

Made in the USA
Charleston, SC
18 January 2015